Values in Education

Notes Toward a Values Philosophy

Max Lerner

VALUES
IN
EDUCATION
Notes Toward a Values Philosophy

By
Max Lerner

PHI DELTA KAPPA
Educational Foundation
Bloomington, Indiana

Perspectives in American Education

This book is one of a five-volume set published by Phi Delta Kappa as part of its national bicentennial year program.
The other titles in the set are:

The Purposes of Education, by Stephen K. Bailey
Alternatives in Education, by Vernon Smith, Robert Barr, and Daniel Burke
Women in Education, by Patricia C. Sexton
Melting of the Ethnics: Education of the Immigrants, 1880–1914, by Mark Krug

To the
youngest generation
in our clan

Timothy Schofield
Matthew Schofield
Daria Russell
Nikki Russell
Betsy Russell
Pamela Townsend
John Townsend
Joshua Lerner

with my dearest wish for them—
Good learning!
Good growing!

Introduction

The two hundredth anniversary of the American declaration of separation from the government of England has stimulated millions of words of sentiment, analysis, nostalgia, and expectation. Much of this verbal and pictorial outpouring has been a kind of patriotic breast-beating. Most of it has been rhetoric.

Several years ago the leadership of Phi Delta Kappa announced its determination to offer a significant contribution to the bicentennial celebration in a series of authoritative statements about major facets of American education that would deserve the attention of serious scholars in education, serve the needs of neophytes in the profession, and survive as an important permanent contribution to the educational literature.

The Board of Directors and staff of Phi Delta Kappa, the Board of Governors of the Phi Delta Kappa Educational Foundation, and the Project '76 Implementation Committee all made important contributions to the creation of the Bicentennial Activities Program, of which this set of books is only one of seven notable projects. The entire program has been made possible by the loyal contributions of dedicated Kappans who volunteered as Minutemen, Patriots, and Bell Ringers according to the size of their donations and by the support of the Educational Foundation, based on the generous bequest of George Reavis. The purpose of the Foundation, as stated at its inception, is to contribute to a better understanding of the educative process and the relation of education to human welfare. These five volumes should serve that purpose well.

A number of persons should be recognized for their contributions to the success of this enterprise. The

Board of Governors of the Foundation, under the leadership of Gordon Swanson, persevered in the early planning stages to insure that the effort would be made. Other members of the board during this period were Edgar Dale, Bessie Gabbard, Arliss Roaden, Howard Soule, Bill Turney, and Ted Gordon, now deceased.

The Project '76 Implementation Committee, which wrestled successfully with the myriad details of planning, financing, and publicizing the seven activities, included David Clark, Jack Frymier, James Walden, Forbis Jordan, and Ted Gordon.

The Board of Directors of Phi Delta Kappa, 1976 to 1978, include President Bill L. Turney, President-Elect Gerald Leischuck, Vice Presidents William K. Poston, Rex K. Reckewey, and Ray Tobiason and District Representatives Gerald L. Berry, Jerome G. Kopp, James York, Cecil K. Phillips, Don Park, Philip G. Meissner, and Carrel Anderson.

The major contributors to this set of five perspectives on American education are of course the authors. They have found time in busy professional schedules to produce substantial and memorable manuscripts, both scholarly and readable. They have things to say about education that are worth saying, and they have said them well. They have made a genuine contribution to the literature, helping to make a fitting contribution to the celebration of two hundred years of national freedom. More importantly, they have articulated ideas so basic to the maintenance of that freedom that they should be read and heeded as valued guidelines for the years ahead, hopefully at least another two hundred.

> —Lowell Rose
> Executive Secretary,
> Phi Delta Kappa

A Personal Note

This book is neither wholly on education nor wholly on values, but on the areas of each where it relates to the other. I trust what emerges is more than the sum of these parts.

I have been a teacher, one way or another, for forty-five years. I have carried the burden of this book with me, as a theme in my thinking, during all those years of the teaching-learning process spent with my students. I have also been an editor and commentator during most of that time—a role less different from the teacher's than most of the practitioners on both sides would admit. Finally, as a father, I have had some experience in helping bring up a brood of children. That is the triple base on which I have sought to build.

A word about the development of my thinking on this base. In my *America as a Civilization* (1957), I had a considerable segment on education, another on the family and the growing-up years in America, and still another on life-purposes and value systems. They belonged, of course, together, but the patterned structure of the book made them seem less related than I had intended. Their relatedness grew in my mind. Five years later I attempted a very brief exploration in my *Education and a Radical Humanism* (1962). I am accordingly grateful to Phi Delta Kappa for a chance to probe further into the interrelations between schooling, family, the growing years, and value formation.

Even the delay was lucky for me. In the intervening years we have learned much about the brain, both in its cognitive and intuitive functioning, and about the double human endowment—creative and destructive—and about what is relatively a "given" and what is learned, about the "reality principle" and the "separate reality," and about both transcendence and immanence in the total cosmos that surrounds the total human being.

Anyone working in the field of education knows how overwhelming the literature is, both on the gut issues and the philosophy. One can hope to do little to add to either except to see them in the context of the discontents and the great civilizational changes of our time. But one finds greater room for fresh thinking on the recent history of values systems in America, on the dynamics of value formation and the dialectical process of changes in value systems. The same is true of democratic elite formation and of the stages of the life cycle as they relate to the exploration of basic life needs.

I have learned much from my encounters with teachers of every kind at their local, state, and national meetings. Because William James had this kind of experience for a number of years, his *Talks to Teachers* was his warmest and most human book. I have learned even more from my students over the years—at Sarah Lawrence, Harvard, Williams, Brandeis, Russell Sage, the University of Florida at Gainesville, and Pomona College.

I have been especially moved by my students in my current seminars at the Graduate School of Human Behavior, U.S. International University, at San Diego. A group of mature men and women, many of them in midcareer, many working and teaching while they learn, they have renewed my belief in the possibility of a joyful classroom, of learning as the growth process of the whole person for the whole life history, and of education as a viable values dialogue.

I add special thanks to Dr. Florence Korn, of Hofstra University and the Roosevelt School, New York, for keeping me alert to trends and changes in the public school system; to my assistant, Carol Hoddeson, who was both prod and shield and who made the manuscript materialize; and to my editor, Donald Robinson, of Phi Delta Kappa, who thought of the book first, shepherded it to the end, and has tried to keep it tolerably free of impurities of style.

Max Lerner

Graduate School of Human Behavior
San Diego, California

Contents

Growth, Change, and Values

The Learning Organism Within its Environments

Education, someone remarked, is what stays with us after everything we were taught has been forgotten. Which implies that learning is deeper and more subtle than teaching, and has ruses and strategies of its own which go beyond the overt intent of most teachers. The teacher seizes a moment in time to transmit his skill or insight, but in the process teacher and learner alike undergo changes. So does the environment within which the learning takes place. Thus there are subtle and complex mirror depths on the whole learning process.

This is my first theme—the fluid, incalculable nature of the teacher-learner experience. It is an interaction of growing organisms in a complex cluster of settings. In this interaction the teacher has a more or less clear design about what he wants to communicate: facts, formulas, skills, techniques, approaches, concepts, insights, values. But time and experience have a withering effect. The facts and formulas fade and have to be replaced, the skills and techniques get antiquated or get changed in practice. Some of the approaches, concepts, and insights leave their mark, transmuted by life experience, yet nonetheless making their impact on a mind and a life. It is the values that stand the best chance of enduring.

What is the crucial element a teacher brings to the learning experience? It is the selfhood of the teacher—a

living personality and character, an image of a functioning man or woman, imperfect, all-too-human, yet
for better or worse a model for the learner.

The learning residue is incalculable exactly because
the experience is a fragile one between a number of
changing and growing organisms in the learning community—teacher, student, other students, other teachers. Often we use the wrong metaphors for what is
involved. We speak of "educating" someone, as if it
is something that someone does to someone or something like feeding or dressing a child, or building
a house. With the new economics we speak of the
"inputs" into education, and the "outputs" that it
results in, just as in the new behaviorism we speak
of "programming" education, as if we were dealing
with an electronic mechanism.

The fact is, of course, that all of education is
organismic, and everyone involved in it is an organism.
One possible metaphor is that of the learning tree.
It has a soil it grows out of, an environment that
nourishes or stunts it, a trunk and branches that reach
up as it grows, leaves that express its energy, an
interaction with everything around it. Learning doesn't
happen within and to and between mechanisms. It
happens within, to, and between organisms.

The tree as metaphor has the weakness of seeming
static. But it is static because it is rooted. Its rootedness
in its soil expresses something of the human rootedness
in man's endowment and environment, and in his
human connections, just as its growth upward—as
it branches out within the circle of its life potential—
expresses something about human aspirations and will.

Human beings have moved beyond the tree because
they have learned to move, and over the millennia
their mobility—in body, voice, gesture, word, and
thought—has grown beyond the wildest early imaginings. This mobility has brought them in touch with
multiple environments, but it has also endangered their
rootedness, and brought in the problem of their root-

lessness to plague them. In addition, by exposing them (on TV, in the illustrated periodicals) to the spectacle of environments which are seductive but outside their options, it has led to frustrations, resentments, and a sense of alienation. At least half the educational task today rests on the need to deal with the life distortions and the broken connections that go with rootlessness and the frustrated sense of inadequacy amidst the plethora of environments.

Hence my subtheme under that of the incalculable nature of the learning experience. *It is incalculable exactly because it deals with organisms enveloped by environments.* The approach of educational thinking has tended to assume a mechano-morphic man—one structured around the metaphor of mechanism. We must posit instead an organismic man, implying the metaphor of organism and environment and the vital relation between them. I might add, as a footnote, that when I speak of metaphorical thinking I might equally be speaking of analogical or paradigmatic thinking. The gradations between metaphor, analogy, and paradigm—all of them phases of the *as if,* some other mode of experience as a model for the experience in question—are less important than the fact of the relationship.

Note here also that the distinction between organism and environment is less sharp than may appear. Learner and teacher—organisms in and to themselves—may be environments to other organisms. What we speak of as environments—the classroom, school, campus, university, family, community, church, neighborhood, gang, peer group—are also in themselves organisms. We have grown so ingrained in the mechano-morphic metaphor that we think of social organisms as "institutions"—established, instituted, lifeless entities. Actually every institution is a maze of habits, attitudes, codes, assumptions, beliefs—ways of conducting life and ways of perceiving life.

Thus the learner and teacher carry on their learning experience as organisms within a number of human and social environments. Some of these are close environments—classroom, school, school yard, family, peer group, ethnic group, neighborhood, media. Others are secondary environments—community, state, government, economy, church, class system, nation, intellectual climate, sexual climate, moral community, the civilization itself, and the world environment of which it is part.

Even the social institutions and communities, which have little of the physiological in them, are nevertheless organismic in the sense that they are subject to growth, change and death, to sickness and health, to deterioration and renewal of vitality. The human learning organisms are likely to be more strongly and deeply affected by their close environments, with which their relationship is more intense, yet a change in a secondary environment—government, the economy, sexual mores, ethnic struggles, women's movements, war, and the draft—may have an intense impact on the learning experience. But even when it does, the fact remains that the learner and teacher can exert fewer controls over their secondary than over their close environments. This difference in the effective exercise of will and intensity may have palpable consequences for the mood and psyche of those involved in the learning experience.

One kind of environment which bears more directly on education than the more distant social organisms is the variety of climates within which the learning takes place. The concept of climates is not an easy one to handle, yet it is a crucial one. There are homes, classrooms, schools, universities, whose climate is austere, crippling, even sick-making. There are others whose climate is genial, expansive, creative. But there is a crucial difference between the climate concept in physical geography and climates in education and society. In the former a climate is pretty much a given—an environment which has changed only over geologic time, and which the organisms must pretty much take as it is. But an intellectual and social climate has more plasticity in it. It is a social creation, the product of human effort, and it can be changed by human effort. This is true of climates in schools and at home, and true also of the climate of ideas, emotions, and values in the larger environments we call society.

Hence one of the most vivid paradoxes of the learning experience—that it takes place within a number of related climates which largely shape what happens in the experience, yet the climates are themselves also the product of that experience. Every encounter in education either confirms or changes something in the intellectual climate. The climate of our own time is largely shaped by the universities and the media, hence the emerging term "media-university complex." Where earlier we thought that power was located in the class system and was forged by class conflict, and later that power was located in the political elites, we now suspect that the elites of media and universities exert a power which in its own way conditions and rivals that of any economic or political group. By shaping the climate of ideas and opinions they become what Shelley called the poets— the "unacknowledged legislators" of their society. I don't go as far as Kevin Phillips goes in calling America a "mediacracy," but no educational theory can afford to underestimate the impact which the climate shaping elites have upon the environment within which learning takes place.

If this organismic approach is valid, it follows that education is centrally concerned with growth—the growth of learner, teacher, society. This is a shorthand way of suggesting a number of purposes which together comprise growth or are linked with it. One is to help in the flowering and fulfillment of personality. Another is to develop a sense of selfhood. Still another is to aid in the effective functioning of both the individual and the society. Finally there is the purpose of helping both of them to a renewal of energy and the transcendence of constrictions.

If growth is the ambiance within which education lives and has its being, transcendence is its metaphysical core. One may speak of the learning experience as a relationship between three elements—student, teacher, and the intellectual tradition and present climate. In this relationship—if it is a healthy one— each grows, and each is transcended.

The Tumults of Change

No society in history has equalled the American in the tumults of change that have swept through it while the educational process has gone on in its midst. These changes, in the past twenty years, have brought a new society into being, a new class alignment, new ethnic, sexual, and generational struggles, a new media power, a new values climate. Any attempt to do justice to their extent and pervasiveness would far outrun the scope of this book. But there is little question of the new influences that bear on the educational experiences, and the difficulty of the questions and tasks being put to it.

From the early Republic, the thrust of American education has been in three directions which first emerged clearly during the watershed period of American educational thinking and organization, in the American Renaissance of the early nineteenth century. One was to shape individuality, a second was to develop national and cultural cohesiveness, a third to strengthen the democratizing forces in the society.

Whatever their differences, the proponents of all three agreed on the overarching institutional means— that schooling in America was to be at once free and compulsory—that is to say, at public expense and by government sanction. It was also to be universal, embracing the young of every class, section, religion. This triad—free, compulsory, and universal public education—has been the mark of t'ie American educational system. It arose out of struggle—between Federalists and Republicans, later between Whigs and Jacksonian Democrats, still later between the propertied and working classes. It had its golden days of triumph from the mid-nineteenth to the mid-twentieth century—roughly from Martin Van Buren's time to Eisenhower's.

More recently, in the wake of the tumults of social change, all three elements of the triad have been challenged. The opponents of financing of free education (notably the economists Henry Simons and Milton Friedman) have argued that education has been hurt, not helped, by being exempted from the larger operation of the free market economy. Whether through the voucher system or some other means, they assert, consumer satisfaction can be better achieved than by a system which seeks the consensus of all and satisfies none. This discontent, largely from the political Right, is strengthened by the conviction on the Left, largely among the more militant ethnic minorities, that their children are not getting the taxpayer's money's worth because the system is tilted toward middle-class whites.

There is also an opposition to the compulsory aspect of education, coming largely from the antistatist libertarians of the Right who regard it as another link in the chain of state servitude. But there is also a group on the Left, led by Ivan Illich, who call for "deschooling" on the ground that schooling interferes with truly functional learning, which should be left to functional class and ethnic groups as group-chosen "tools for conviviality."

Finally, there is an attack on universality in education, on the ground that the present schooling is of more doubtful benefit to some groups than to others, that the game is rigged by the possessing groups against the financially deprived ones, that the local school financing base operates inequitably because it favors the children of wealthier localities, and that the total

American educational system, with its rhetoric of
freedom and universalism, is a screen behind which
the possessors manipulate and propagandize the children of the disinherited. Most of this comes from the
Left. But the struggles over the busing of students
in the lower and middle schools, and over the quota
system in higher education, have also stirred a conservative revolt against the lively force of universal
education and the tyranny of a school system which
is conscripted into use as an engine for radical social
change.

The fact of such attacks is not new. But their nature
changes with the changing social climates and their
intensity increases with the accelerations of social
change. I shall return in the next section to some
of the questions I have raised above. What I want
to note here is that the attacks on the public school
system, whatever their validity in fact, are built into
the nature of the system and the society. They are
part of the decision-making process in a dynamic
democracy which has become a pressure-group democracy.

No idyllic school-on-a-hill here. Schooling and the
schools are caught up in all the anguish of social
struggle around them. The antiwar and antidraft
struggles of the 1960s were fought out largely on
college campuses and in college classrooms and corridors. The ethnic rebellions, among blacks, Chicanos,
Puerto Ricans, and American Indians, were similarly
fought out in the local school districts as well as in
the colleges, which became arenas of activisms that
took the issues of desegregation and busing from the
local communities to the Supreme Court—and back
again. The ecological campaigns against pollutions
and for environmental protection largely had their
origins among the young, many of whom learned
something about the relation between theory and
action by working within these movements. This
proved even truer of the women's liberation movement,

which found eager participants as well as believers among high school and college students, and which deeply affected the curriculum, teaching staff, and value system in the schools.

In short, the relationship between school and society, which John Dewey had written about, ceased to be an academic question to be thrashed out among the educational philosophers. It became a clamorous present reality, forcing itself urgently for resolution on teachers, administrators, and parents and posing new problems for politicians and judges.

This happened not only with the political and ethnic activisms of the 1960s and early 1970s, but with the institutional and cultural revolutions as well. The family was subjected to an unprecedented battering, from the generational revolt, the women's movement, the economic changes, and the revolutions in sexual attitudes and behavior as well as the research into sexuality. There were new awareness and encounter movements, consciousness-heightening movements, and a transpersonal research into a "separate reality." New life-styles and personality styles were discussed and emerged. The traditional value codes came under intensified attack, and new challenger value codes made their bid for acceptance. In fact, the values debate—along with the concept of alternative life-styles and alternative ways of perceiving reality—may have done even more to shake up the educational system and philosophy than all the political and ethnic activisms. The school is related to society in subtler and more elusive ways than many educational philosophies have been willing to concede.

This then is the situation of learning in a dynamic democracy, of education caught between the winds of change in the society and the strong new currents in the culture. Before a frame for learning can be agreed on, there must be a consensus on where, when, how, with whom, by whom, at whose cost, by what means, and toward what goals the young will be educated. Nowhere else in the world is there, to the same extent, the conviction that education is a battleground in which all the forces loose in the society are engaged in struggle, that a democracy must battle about education even while it is educating. The classroom is set within an arena, and in fact itself becames an arena for some of these warring elements—an angry classroom in an angry society.

Thus the Marxist idea that the schools must educate for revolutions becomes absurd in the American setting. For the American schools are already deeply enmeshed in whatever revolutions have been around. I use the term "revolution" not in the classical sense of hard-core revolutions of violence within a frame of ideology, but in the deeper sense of the accelerated movements of change in a society, in great periods of social transformation. The 1960s were such a revolutionary decade. In the dynamics of social change there are laws of acceleration and deceleration. One can make an attempt to get at the first by using the changes of the 1960s as a case history, and also to get at the second by using the first half of the 1970s similarly. Educational thinkers must on this score become students of the pace swings and mood swings of the civilization as a whole, if they are to achieve a perspective of the total learning environment, and see the difference between where education is moving and where it ought to move.

The sixties were a traumatic experience not only for the university campuses that were the scene of the major dislocations and upheavals, but for the whole educational system. They seemed to many a nest of scorpions. In some ways America during that decade experienced what Yeats may have meant to convey in his "Second Coming":

A blood-dimmed tide is loosed upon the world.
The ceremony of innocence is drowned.

In its own American fashion it had some of the characteristics of the Cultural Revolution which took place in China at roughly the same time—in the latter half of the 1960s. There were similar stirrings-up among the young, a similar generational distance between the young and less young, a similar competition of militancies, similar attacks by "Red Guards"— or their equivalents—upon the established bureaucracies, a similar cult of violence using the quickened activisms as their screen, and a similar danger that education itself would get lost among the urgencies of the immediate moment.

The crucial difference was that the Red Guards did what they did because they were imbued with a belief system which came to them presumably from Marx and Lenin, mediated of course through the "correct" thoughts of Mao Tse-tung, while in the American case the young did what they did exactly because the traditional belief system had broken down, and they were seeking a new—and more credible—one.

The irony, at least in America, was that the great dream of liberal educational thinkers came true in the sixties, yet those who had dreamt it had the feeling that the dream was dreaming them. I am speaking of the dream of "education for social change," which stretched beyond Dewey all the way back to Channing, Alcott, and Parker. All along American educators had hoped they could bring about changes in the society as well as in the individual students. When it did happen there was little agreement about what it had meant and what residue it would leave.

Whatever the distortions of the dream—and they are there and they are serious—one aspect of it must not be overlooked. It is the fact of a society in total process of education.

Three out of four American children finish high school. I am not saying they finish it well. They don't. In many cases their skills are defective, their insights minimal, their values twisted. Many who will go on to college—and those numbers are also mounting— will not be well prepared. But what counts here is

their society's concern with them, which furnishes
the frame by which inadequacies are gauged. A primary
school system which copes with misfits and sick
children as well as with healthy, a system of high
schools cutting across class and ethnic lines (14 percent
of the high achievers in senior year come from the
lower economic classes) which have become "People's
Colleges," a system of higher education oriented increasingly toward mass education even while it struggles with the shaping of elites, a cluster of media
and other nonschool and extraschool educational
agencies: these are the evidences of a society in total
process of education.

Think of me, Lyndon Johnson used to plead, as
an "education President." Were it not for the Vietnam
war, this fact about him would be less obscured than
it is. The society Johnson presided over was an education society. It will be true of every President to come.

But an open society in total process of education
is also bound to be one in total process of change,
of skepticism, of discontents, of value conflict and
confusion. This may define some of the problems
ahead for the civilization.

Education can be a cohesive force in a society, as
it was in an earlier America, or it can be a dissolvent
force, as it has been in the past half century. When
there was some clarity about both the ends and means
of education its impact on the nation was a stabilizing
one. The whole society—school, family, church, community, work—was a learning and value-instilling
experience that moved the young along a well-defined
life-view and life cycle. De Tocqueville saw this when
he noted not only the specific schooling institutions
(*les lumieres*) but also the "civil religion" which made
the whole society a learning and cohering environment.
But when most of the forces in the society—science,
technology, industrialism, rationalism, secularism,
specialization—are disintegrative forces, then the
schools (which are societies in embryo) reflect them,

and the total impact is corrosive of both cohesion and belief.

Yet curiously the people in the society expect the schools to act as the final fortress, remaining firm even as the cracks are opening up in the society around it. The fact is that the family, the churches, the neighborhood, the community, the party system, the class and ethnic systems, the legal and sexual codes, the value system, have all been subjected to an intensive battering. So have the schools. Yet with a real confusion about what the schools can and can't do, many people expect them to assume the burdens which the other institutions have faltered in bearing—to inherit the tasks which the others have laid down and become the residuary legatees of social obligation, in effect receivers in bankruptcy.

The Fiery Centrality of Values

At times a debate has raged about whether education should be concerned with values. It is an idiot debate in that form, on a hopelessly archaic question. As well ask whether religion should be concerned with the problem of godhead. Every actor in the educational drama—teacher, student, family, administrator, media, peer group—is up to its neck in values. Like it or not, education is values-drenched. The real question is how well—with what awareness, with what skill and meaning, with what responsibility and restraint—it performs its function as value carrier.

The term *value* itself, in this context, is often used with two meanings which are linked but which need nonetheless to be distinguished. In ethics, as in economics, value means essentially *worth*. What is it that makes life worth living? What are the guiding life purposes that give meaning to life?

Those are aspects of the first use of the value concept. The second is related, but with a different thrust. It is best illustrated by the well-worn story of Gertrude Stein on her deathbed, asking, "What is the answer?"—"I am afraid we don't know."—"Well then, what is the question?" Values are the crucial questions we put to life, not only explicitly by philosophic probing, but implicitly by the way we live.

While not scanting the first meaning of *value,* my emphasis is on the second because it underscores the element of quest. Not every life question refers to a value, but every value implies a life question. It is a question about the strivings, commitments, and beliefs that give meaning to what might otherwise remain a tale told by an idiot, full of sound and fury, signifying little.

Viewed thus, man is not only a political, economic, and social animal, but a valuing animal. Aristotle felt that man could not live outside the *polis*—the human community. But neither can he live outside his valuing function, in the values community. It is like an atmosphere, an ambiance, the sea he swims in. It may also be—to use Simon Bolivar's historic disillusioned phrase about revolutions—the sea he ploughs.

If values are, as I see them, questions we put to life, and therefore meanings we strive for, then they go beyond factual or scientific knowledge, beyond reasoning power, beyond skills and masteries, which have been regarded as the heart of education but which don't disclose their full import unless they are directed to the shaping and service of values. A life without values is an empty life, a life with unformed or distorted values is a warped one. Education is not meant to lead to empty or warped lives but to lives as full as we can make them. Hence the fiery centrality of values in education.

How then has it happened that values teaching has been neglected in American public education? An answer may lie in five historical directions.

First, the churches tainted values teaching as parochial. In colonial America and the early Republic, values found their way into the schools mainly as religious instruction. As a result, they were tainted for later generations. The teaching of values was edged with taboo, especially for liberals, for whom the Madisonian wall of separation between church and state was a passionate principle of education.

Second, politics tainted values teaching as partisan. When Federalist and Jeffersonian, Whig and Jacksonian schoolmasters alike taught moral philosophy, the driving wedge of partisan politics was never far away. Even Jefferson, from our perspective the great libertarian, was careful to protect the students at his cherished new University of Virginia from the corrupting blight of Federalist heresies imbedded in dangerous textbooks and teachers. Here was America's first Philosopher-King, who detested monarchy and was suspicious of all philosophical systems. Yet as a philosopher he knew the power of ideas, and as a politician he knew they could be distorted for partisan purposes. Hence he was wary of the teaching of values implicit in all teaching. His own solution was not to stay clear of values teaching, but to get the right partisans—Whigs and Jeffersonians, of course—to fill the teaching posts.

Later generations, imbued with the fear of partisan values as well as theological ones, tended to shun the whole problem. The fact that sectional values, both before and after the Civil War, found their way into the textbooks and classroom, made it even more imperative to make a detour around the values problem.

Third, the home and other institutions preempted much of the values task. I have spoken of de Tocqueville who knew as well as anyone the religious as well as the political interests of Americans. Yet he didn't put much stress on their formal education—the enlightenment and instruction which he called *les lumieres.* He saw the whole functional process of community living as the real educational process. It comprised the town meetings, the jury system, the voluntary and self-improvement organizations, the political parties and their meetings and newspapers,

the impassioned discussions at inns and wherever
people met, and most of all the home itself. This was
where the *moeurs* were shaped—the mores, attitudes,
customs, values—which became a civic religion, and
this civic religion was what gave American society
in the early Republic some of the cohesion it had.

It was nothing less than an embedded value system
which, as the nation was settled on the moving frontier,
became in effect a portable value system. De Tocqueville was excited by the image of the pioneer "plunging
into the wilderness of the New World, with his Bible,
axe, and newspapers"—that is to say, with religious
belief, with a clearing tool for a home, and with civic
ideas. In their growing-up years the young Americans
internalized the values implicit in it, especially in the
home. The daughters were as clearly shaped by it
as the sons, and much of the vigor and independence
of the American woman came out of it, rather than
out of any system of school instruction. When sons
and daughters broke away from the home, moving
often to a new community farther West, it was not
an act of alienation but one of starting new homes
and communities within a context that blended elements of the earlier ethos with a new environment.

Fourth, the dominant pragmatism interfered. With
the triumph of industrialism the practical men who
ran the school districts found little that was usable
in values education. They favored the more productive
and vendible phases of education, trusting the schools
to bring the children of the immigrant families into
the melting pot and make the society cohesive. But
the main thrust of the values task was left to home
and church.

Fifth, the dominant educational establishment bun-
gled it. Under the pressure of rebel liberal educators,
reacting against the dry as dust tradition, the movement
for the teaching of values came to be associated with
"life adjustment" concepts of "progressive" education.
This pleased neither the conservatives, who placed

their stress on "basics" and "essentials" and derided the new trend, nor the intellectual sophisticates who felt that it would lead to consensus and conformity rather than to the "new social order" they aimed at.

This historical experience suggests something about values in education which has been too often ignored. The value teaching task has to be done, but it is as foolish to say that the school has no business in it as it is to say that it should be the school's only business, or that party and creed should use the school as a values instrument for their purposes.

Actually there is a values setting—a web of relationships which crisscross in the life experience of the student, and which together shape his values, whether deliberately or not.

The family of origin is the central relationship in that cluster. It has in the past done more in value formation—and more deliberately—than it does now, but as long as it holds together it will remain the chief agent acting on the child in his most formative years.

The school ought to be the second agent, but in many—perhaps in most—cases it is a weakened second. The reason is that in part it has been stripped of a number of its former roles, especially in discipline and dress codes. But there is a broader reason. Having gone on the defensive because of its loss of authority, the school went along with the total climate of permissiveness. But this permissiveness in turn pushed it further on the defensive and weakened its authority even more.

In the past the school was at core an instrument of civic education, in the sense of shaping civic loyalties—toward law, the government, and the basic political traditions. But latterly, both in the slums and the suburbs, youngsters in the elementary and high schools developed what is at best an ambivalent attitude toward authority and loyalty. The antiwar and antidraft protests were the first to break through the surface coating of authority. They were followed by Watergate and the revelations about the intelligence agencies, and the resulting obsession with "conspiracies" retroactively cast doubt on the assassination episodes of the 1960s and raised the question whether anyone could believe the authenticity of anything that had happened. This is not a context in which a value-shaping agency can have much effectiveness.

If the school is yielding some of its influence, there are two other elements of the values setting which have gained in importance. One is the network of intimacy relationships, as distinguished from the formal learning relationships. The other is the sense of generational consciousness. Both of them overlap with the first two settings, of school and family: in each of the latter settings there are friendship and sexual intimacies, and in each of them also a sense of separateness from other generations.

Yet beyond the overlapping, the burden of shaping both personal intimacy and generational identity is carried by the peer group, which now makes a bid to be recognized in educational theory as a major and integral part of the value-creating process. Where the traditional agencies—family, school, church, government, law—have had to yield a good deal of their authority, the peer group has strengthened its hold on the young. Whether this is a healthy direction is debatable: friendship, love, sexuality, and mental health have more to gain from bridge-building between the generations than from isolation. I use peer group here not only for the young, but for all one-generational groups, including the narrow friendship and social groups of married people. But whatever one's view, it is important to recognize the peer group as a force in both sets of relationships.

The fifth setting is in work relationships, using *work* in the broadest sense of vocation, or calling, rather than in the narrower sense of the job. In traditional theory, work has been seen as part of the life for which education is a preparation. But from the angle of values-formation, work is a phase of education as well as of life, and—whether during or after the formal schooling—the work community (shop, farm, office, factory, hospital, laboratory, hangar, orchestra) is a crucial phase of values-formation, continuance, and change. Unfortunately it has not been recognized as such, either by educational thinkers or the larger public, to the impoverishment of theory and the confusion of practice. From the values standpoint work may be more crucial to education than the cognitive aspect of schooling is, since it is woven into the daily round of existence and becomes integrated with the unconscious life rhythms.

Logically, following the work setting, the sixth should be the play relationship. But it is a commentary on the society of "grown-ups" that the play concept does not survive the onset of maturity, nor are there play communities in the sense that there are work communities. In its place we talk of leisure, more in the Greek sense of nonwork and of time on our hands than in the sense of time available for work and play alike.

My own preference, in place of leisure, is for the concept of exploration. I mean the exploring of the world beyond the intimate and face-to-face relations of love, friendship, sexuality, and work: the effort to use the media, recreation, and travel for more random exploration. We have not yet begun to take the measure of the importance which our adventures in the press, TV, film, sports, music, the arts, holiday experiences, and travel have—separately and together—in the formation of values. Exploration as a values setting has itself been little explored and recognized. Yet exactly because we feel ourselves relaxed rather than committed as we explore the world beyond our imme-diate relationships, exactly because it seems random rather than purposive ("not to eat, not for love, but only gliding, gliding"), the censor within us is off-guard, and the identifications that are set up can become important. It is in this area that we try out roles less practiced than in the work, school, and family aspects of our lives.

I move now, for the seventh value setting, to the inward journeys that every person must make—all through life, but increasingly with every added year— into the nature of the mystery of self, society, existence, being, godhead, transcendence. The techniques may be those affecting awareness, consciousness levels, meditation, bio-feedback, body and mind control, the perception of levels of reality. But whatever the techniques, and however they may shift—as they do—from era to era and from one climate of ideas and experience to another, the inescapable fact is that the reality behind them is at the very core of our lives.

Because the inward journeys form part of what is for each person, however inchoately or stumblingly, the nub of meaning, they form a setting for values shaping and consolidation, whether as religion, faith, commitment, mystique, or belief system. Without this values setting it would be hard to understand any of the core experiences that give education its dimension and meaning and to which in turn education tries to give definition. To call these, as Maslow does, peak-experiences is to overstress the sensory and the conscious in them. I prefer the term *core experiences* or—from another standpoint—*meaning systems.* As with each of the other six relationships, they not only express values but also furnish a setting for shaping values.

All seven of these values settings together bring us back to the classical question from which every theory of education must start: How can human beings—"poor, forked radishes," all of us, with "heads fantastically carved"—learn and grow in such a way that our jumbled lives, our mutilated psyches, our dangerous endowment, our stumbling blunder-beset lives can gain more meaning? How can we get help, from others and from ourselves, so that the lives we lead will enable us to put better questions to life, and those questions in turn will enable us to lead lives with less psychic brutality and less moral squalor?

It is because this question is so central that we must bring to bear on it what I have spoken of as the fiery centrality of values.

The Realm of Theory

The Double Endowment

It is an almost forgotten fact that the American school system came into being at roughly the same time—from the 1830s through the 1850s—that the idea of "civilized morality" was transported from Great Britain to America and consolidated here. The two have gone hand in hand ever since—a sequence of efforts to build an ideal school system along with a complacent view of the nature of the beast, of the basic human endowment on which every educational superstructure has to build.

There has been all along a grave dysjunction between the two. The models on which Americans built their view of the human endowment—the early Calvinist model, the Jeffersonian model, the neo-Calvinist (Victorian) model, the Darwinian model, the pragmatic model, the Freudian model—have come variously from theology, science, political and economic myth, philosophy, psychology. The movements for school reform have come out of the felt needs of the people themselves, but have been carried out within the intellectual climate expressed by the models or paradigms.

The state of the theory and the state of the art of education have often been discordant. If Americans have largely done better with the art than with the theory it is because their optimism has driven them constantly to great efforts at educational action, but their accompanying tender-mindedness has kept them from facing the Medusa-head of the nature of the beast, and has thus kept their educational theory crippled.

Borrowing from seventeenth-century British theology the idea of the "fortunate fall"—the good luck of the expulsion from the Garden, which confronted men with the necessity for moral choice—one may speak of the fortunate fall in American intellectual history which confronted educational thinkers with the need to make intellectual choices. The social convulsions of the late 1950s, the 1960s, and the early 1970s may have furnished a frame for a more tough-minded view of the human endowment.

Fortunately also we have a chance to rethink the nature of the beast at a time of intense intellectual revolution which has brought with it new insights into psychology, psychotherapy, brain research, genetics, sexual research, linguistics, ethology, comparative civilization theory, and in general the bio-socio-psychological disciplines. New questions are being put to education because they are being put to collective living. New knowledge and insights are available to education because they are available to collective living. The insights from all past knowledge, experiment, and experience are accessible to us to a degree never true before. If we do not avail ourselves of them it will be because we are too immersed in anxieties, fears, and self-doubts to allow our collective intelligence to free itself for the task.

The need to bring up and educate the young, at great expense and trouble, is based on the Eros principle, which includes parental love and concern. But it is also based in part on the yearning for immortality, through children and the continuity of the family. But the question still remains about how educable any of us are, young and older alike—what the chances and limits of learning are. To get a sense of the problem

one might take a book like Fred and Grace Hechinger's
Growing Up in America, a fine product of the James-
Deweyite main current of the American tradition,
tempered by good sense yet basically optimistic, and
set alongside it any book by Robert Ardrey on man's
animal inheritance, or a summary of recent research
into psycho-social traits in man, like Anthony Storr's
brief survey, *Human Destructiveness.*

On the whole, Americans, with all their worship
of Nature, have opted for the power of nurture in
shaping personality and character. They have not
believed with Saint-Exupery that the ultimate triumph
is "the triumph of the seed." They believe it is the
triumph of correct child care. They don't believe, with
writers like Konrad Lorenz, that 80 or 90 percent of
what happens to individuals, and indeed to a society,
is due to genetic factors: they believe in the social
factors. They recognize the fact of biological evolution,
but they put more stress on social and cultural evolution.

Americans know the force of the instinctual and
nonrational, but they prefer to believe that the cognitive and the rational are the governors of life. They
pay homage to the right brain but they put their trust
in the left brain. They talk of limits but their faith
is in plasticity. They set store by the organismic but
they operate on the engineering principle—not only
technologically but socially. They have a comic genius
as well as a practical one, but have always averted
their eyes from the tragic mask of life. Since they
believe that happiness is a natural right they cannot,
in Freud's terms, be content with the assumption that
the price of civilization is the acceptance of happiness
reduction. They make a cult of the future and deny
death. They make a cult of children and push aside
the elderly. Their religions give prominence to the
adversary, yet their conception of human nature leaves
little room for the force of evil and of the destructive.

I am aware that this portrait of the metaphysical
assumptions by which Americans think and live is

at once incomplete and too simplified, yet I offer it
as a rough approximation. As it happens, it is a better
portrait of the American liberal strain than of the
conservative. The latter is more likely, in his political
theology, to believe that all government is evil, but
his faith in laissez-faire belies his belief that human
nature also is evil. In fact the current battle in American
education, between the liberals, who favor expressiveness and the spontaneous for the child, and the
conservatives, who favor stress on discipline, the
"basics," and the "essentials," has more sound and
fury in it than depth of meaning. The two groups
disagree on means, but they share a common assumption of the plasticity of the human endowment and
therefore of the child's educability. American educational   theory—whether   Calvinist,   Jeffersonian,
pragmatic, evolutionary, even Freudian—has always
operated on that assumption.

My own impulse is to refuse to accept the either-or
frame of most of the dualisms I have cited. Moral
choices may move between *either* and *or,* but organismic life itself—for the social as well as the individual
organism—runs in terms of *both-and.* The human
organism contains both body and brain, both hemi-
spheres of the brain, both cognition and feeling. The
human endowment, coming down from the hominoids
through all the centuries of adaptation and selection,
is a double endowment. It includes within itself all
the crucial contradictions that make the human family
what it is. It is not monolithic. It is a battlefield on
which all the battles of humanity have been fought
out and are still being fought out.

The human species is neither diabolical nor angelic.
It has elements of both built into it, and it has further
elements of each which are potential, and whose
outcome depends on family nurture, social conditioning, and individual will.

I don't use "potential" here in the familar sense
in which it is used so optimistically in human potential

psychology, and still less do I use it to suggest that human nature is an instinctless *tabula rasa* on which the rational intelligence of society and the individual can write some utopian message. Utopias deal with perfections, and the human endowment as we have it is terribly imperfect. Utopias also require thought police, so that the perfect human endowment can be kept perfect. I speak rather of a human nature which does have built-in drives and propensities that we must reckon with, and contradictions we must grapple with. But there remains a frame, whose extent we cannot know, within which social intelligence and human will can function in sorting out the potentials and giving them direction.

My own propensity is neither toward pessimism nor optimism about the human endowment, but toward possibilism. It is as a possibilist—wary, critical, yet hopeful—that I approach the bundles of potentials which come within the frame of whatever is so built-in by the past that it seems unalterable, whatever therefore we must accept as givens, but which are themselves still plastic enough to be subject to direction, channeling, change.

An instance of this will be found in the question of human aggression and destructiveness—man's aggressive-destructive drive. All the evidence, in history and in contemporary life, points to the presence of this drive as deeply imbedded in the human endowment. One may attribute it to Original Sin or to man's hominoid inheritance as a primate, but whatever the original impetus, the harsh fact remains that is embodied in the Latin phrase—*homo homini lupus:* man is a wolf to man.

In fact, some of the defenders of the nonhuman animals resent the comparison. They point out that animals kill for food, not for sport or for ideology. In fact, the very quality of advance in the size and complexity of the human brain over millions of years, the increase in cognivitve and conceptual capacity,

man's soaring imagination, his ability to build impressive constructions of words, ideas, and symbols—this
very quality, which Bronowski has celebrated in his
Ascent of Man, giving it a Darwinian reverse twist,
has also acted as a multiplier of his destructiveness.
Not only can the new weapons technology kill in the
millions where the earlier ones killed only in the
thousands, but the killings come out of conceptual
fanatacisms (ideologies) which get to be rationalized
as sacred obligations to kill.

On a lesser scale and plane than this mass destructiveness, human life, in its interpersonal encounters
and relations, offers countless daily examples of individual aggression and destructiveness in man's inhu-
manity to man.

There have been some thinkers and teachers who,
in their recoil from these dark recesses of the human
psyche, have jumped back either to a denial of the
aggressive-destructive element and a belief that it is
always socially created, or to a conviction that all
aggressivity is destructive. Both would be fatal to the
theory and art of education. There is, in aggression,
an element of forward thrust without which human
beings might settle into an unchanging torpor. No
meaningful social advance or personal energy can
operate without at least a tincture of it. The Greeks,
who were highly competitive and tolerated only the
winners in any contest, called it *agon,* for the wrestler
as symbol of the constant Greek effort at transcendence. Nietzsche, who studied Socrates as an
educator, was obsessed with it. He welcomed energy,
wrestling, conflict, testing: "What does not destroy
me strengthens me," he wrote. The teacher or parent
who sets out to flatten and extinguish this energy in
the young does himself—and society—a disservice.

The destructive aspect of aggression is quite another
thing. Students of child development have distinguished between the crying of an infant which is
expressive of animal spirits, a call for attention, and

an assertion of *being there,* and the rage crying which expresses deprivation, acute discomfort, lack of love and security, fear of the environment. Such rages are warning cries of the germination of what will later become murderous or self-destructive, or both.

The fact about the double endowment is that, along with human destructiveness, there is also a human creativeness built into the species, and to varying degrees into every individual, if only it can somehow be released. It may express itself in artifacts of great moment or in creative decision making or in a kindling quality in the ordinary relations of homemaking and daily life. Or it may get dammed up, or misdirected, or distorted into destructiveness. We still know relatively little about the nature of the creative process— about its sources, its encounters, how it is triggered, how it transforms experience, emotion, and imagination into something that didn't exist before.

There are some who believe that education can do little with it, except perhaps to hurt it, and should therefore leave it alone. Others believe that education has no business with it anyway, since its goals are national and social, or else practical, rather than individual fulfillment. I challenge both. The fact that it has often done badly with creative potentials doesn't mean that it can't do better. The fact that it *also* has national and social goals doesn't mean that it excludes the developmental ones, which are its crucial task.

A word finally—after the destructive and the creative—about the social in the human endowment. Education does its work within the context of human communities and not in isolation. It must use whatever base it can find in the human endowment which it can use to strengthen the social bond while it helps discover the diverse individuality of each student.

I call this the *nexus* which links human being to human being. The theorists of the "social contract"— Hobbes, Locke, Rousseau—promised some time in history when men gave up a share of their freedom in order to get the protection of the state and law. The current premise is that some bent for living together—call it *civility* rather than contract—comes built into the human endowment, however skimpy or fragile it may be. In terms of the values-shaping process, education must be as concerned with civility as with destructiveness and creativeness.

There is nothing about human development, about history and society, about the intricacies of the psyche and the mysteries of the cosmos, that should be alien to the theory and art of education. To be at once teacher and learner is the most consuming vocation—and the most dangerous, for it deals with the values that either give life meaning or make nonsense of it.

Clusters of Human Needs

What are the basic human needs? There has been much talk of the aims and goals of education which has suffered from a failure to explore, if not finally to establish, the nature of human needs.

Much of the material for such an effort must come from developmental psychology: what is it that the developing human organism cannot get along *without?* Accordingly a number of insights also come from the theory and practice of psychotherapy, with damaged psyches and distorted lives. But we cannot be content with the approach only through privations and pathologies. What is it whose presence and full use makes human lives satisfying and creative?

If we can arrive at some clarity on this score, it may serve as an added base—supplementing the inquiry into the human endowment—for a greater clarity on the human values that education must reckon with.

I have tried in my own teaching to discuss with my students their perception of human needs, taken empirically from their own lives and their work with others. Matching their insights with my own experience, and with what emerges from the literature, I suggest the following seven clusters of basic needs.

It would be idle to set them down in any order of importance. There can be no *hierarchy* of needs where all are crucial for the function of the organism. I am also aware of the inevitable overlappings. But they may serve as a frame for evaluating a good deal in the theory and art of education. I should add that each of the seven is itself a cluster of related needs. For each I have chosen a single term as central to the rest, but the reader may find some other term in each cluster more illuminating.

1) The need for *growth.* I stress here the adaptability of the organism to the new environments and situations, its flexible capacity to change and to accept change. There is a related need for freedom—the freedom to explore, to experiment, to make mistakes and try again. This involves in turn the need for making choices and decisions from available life options—as also the need for having the options there, instead of isolation and a sense of entrapment.

I must add however that growth does not flourish in a situation of formlessness and anarchy. For healthy growth an organism needs not only freedom but a sense of limits. Adaptability means little unless there is a given, to adapt to. Flexible change would mean chaos unless there were also continuities. Choices and decisions would also lose meaning if the options were limitless: it is the fact of limits that makes the choices growth-producing. An organism without limits would go berserk. Growth without limits becomes a metastasis.

2) The need for *security,* which is as important for healthy functioning as the need for freedom. The human organism, living in a world of chance and danger, needs to feel secure against hostile invasions either from the known or the unknown. This need to feel secure is one of the reasons why the human organism needs structure and order. The passion for order can become rigidity, which inhibits growth and

the adaptation to change. But there can be security without growing rigid, which becomes a kind of death-in-life. The essence of security lies in boundaries which guard the organism against intrusions from without, while at the same time they give the self some definition and release its capacity for growth without paralyzing fears.

3) The need for *selfhood* or *identity*. Every organism has at some point been part of another, and by individuation has become a characteristic and unique self. This is truer of the human organism than of any other, because the awareness of self is sharper among humans, and because—especially in the Western tradition—a special value attaches to being oneself, not someone else, not part of an undistinguishable mass. The quest for identity—the search for the authentic self—is not a one-time episode, over with as soon as it is achieved. It is a continuing process in the course of the life cycle, which becomes a kind of stations-of-the cross journey: at each stage selfhood needs to be reestablished, uniqueness needs to be reaffirmed, the boundaries dividing oneself from others need to be redefined.

4) The need for *belonging*. The reader will note that the first two human needs—growth and security—formed an interacting pair. The same is true of the second pair—selfhood and belonging. One might almost say selfhood and otherhood.

Selfhood must have limits: carried all the way it becomes solipsism. Individualism has its corruptions, always tending toward the sterility and the swollen pride of the "imperial I." In the long history of biological evolution the selection process, operating through genetic competition, has stressed selfhood—a kind of biological selfishness. But the history of social and cultural evolution produced a counter-tendency, toward altruism, a concern about what happens to others. Human beings need not only to feel cared *for:* they need also to *care.* The isolated individual, unloving, unable to receive love, dries up and withers. He needs to feel that he is one with others—what Robert Nisbet has called the *social bond* and what I prefer to call the *human nexus.*

In ant colonies the sense of individuality has been eliminated, and all that remains is membership in the larger group. In human societies, especially in urbanized open societies, the opposite is more nearly true. The sharp unsatisfied need is the sense of belonging. When too long unfulfilled it can be distorted into the "obedience to authority" pattern that Milgram noted in his simulated cruelty experiments and can lead to the mystique of a totalitarian society.

5) The need for *meaning.* This may take many forms, which will vary with the moral and values climate in a particular society and time. In the West the need for meaning has expressed itself in *struggle* and what goes with it—coping, *agon,* the sense of danger and hard ground, the stretching of self under difficulty; and also in a striving for *achievement* and *recognition.* In the East it has expressed itself in inner rather than outer striving, in *being* rather than achieving, sometimes even in the obliteration of self in order to find deeper levels of consciousness and self-discipline.

Yet what is common to these contrasting modes of expression is the need for meaning which is unique to the human organism, and which persists even in the most extreme situations, at the peril of concluding that one's existence had left no imprint on an indifferent and uncomprehending cosmos.

6) The need for *feeling* and *interacting* with other human beings and with all the environments available. This has recently been put in terms of awareness and encounter, earlier in terms of "interpersonal relations," but the terms may prove transitory while the need they express is permanent. Work, play, love, conversing, art—all the basic life functionings are phases of the need for interacting, while feeling is what gives

the interactions their depth and richness, lest they
become forms of a lifeless, abominable puppetry. We
have talked much recently about *fulfillment,* not in
the sense of perfect happiness or life expressiveness—
which are counsels of impossibility—but in the sense
of fullness of living ("a full life," we often say). But
fulfillment is not a human need: it is only a far-off
goal, a giant yardstick by which to measure the *degree*
of richness and expressiveness of living that it is
possible for humans to attain.

7) The need for *believing.* This is related to the
need for belonging, discussed earlier, in the sense
that both are stretching of selves beyond self, in one
case to become part of something that will be suppor-
tive of self, in the other to find something one can
support, not only beyond self but sometimes beyond
cognition, reason, validation, even beyond perception
and understanding. Belief is whatever you put your
stakes on, whatever it is that moves humans to their
actions and their passions. The object of belief is
varied—God, country, history, dialectical materialism,
love, freedom, sacred writings, the mission of a people
or race. But its essence lies in mystery and faith—the
mysterium tremendum that theologians have fixed on,
the faith which needs no final validation because its
sacral quality carries validation with it.

I have listed above a random collection of objects
and symbols of belief. But what counts even more
than assorted beliefs is a constellation of beliefs—a
belief system, sometimes with a religious, sometimes
with an ideological base. There is no human need
for belief systems, such as Christianity, or Buddhism,
or magic, or the Chinese variant of Marxism. But it
is the human need for believing that makes the belief
systems possible.

Using the same approach, and surveying all seven
of the needs I have listed and discussed, one may
say that human beings have needs, but their en-
compassing need is for a need system which brings

them all together into a constellation. Man is a growing animal, a security- and identity-seeking animal, a belonging animal, a meaning-seeking animal, a feeling/interacting animal, a believing animal. *Each of these phases of his being and striving is the source of his search for values related to that phase.* And each cluster of these values searchings—and all of them together—become the central concern and indeed the substance of the curiously fumbling, painful, joyful developmental Pilgrim's Progress that we call an education.

Growing Up and Growing

Within this frame of the human endowment and human needs, the developmental story has played itself out on the stage of every society. The enactment of it takes diverse forms in diverse societies. In America, given an open society, a competitive tradition, an achievement orientation, a sense of plenty, and a cult of the child, the crucial conflict has been between *growing up* (in the "right" way) and *growing* (in the child's—and later the man's or woman's—own way).

The little two-letter word, *up,* is responsible for considerable grief in educational and social theory. Everything in America is child-oriented, and so is education. There is nothing wrong, and there is everything right, in speaking of the growing up years—as I did in a section of *America as a Civilization*—as a crucial phase of the life cycle. Fred and Grace Hechinger developed the theme much more fully in their *Growing Up in America* (1975), as did Robert Coles in a Bicentennial essay for *Time* with the same title. Erik Erikson dealt with the same material, more psychoanalytically, in his *Childhood and Society,* and indeed a whole psychological knowledge industry has clustered around the rubric of child development.

The difficulty comes when educational thinking—and practice—are drawn fatefully into the orbit of the growing up concept, and limited to that. A number of able writers on education, including the Hechingers, have not wholly escaped this suction force. Because education is *centrally* concerned with the growing up years, when the mind and personality are malleable, it doesn't follow that it must be *exclusively* concerned with these years. Even those who take the longer view, and see education as a continuing force in a total life history, tend to see the later years within the intense circle of light cast on them by early education. But the opposite is just as true—that what happens to the growth of the mind, personality, and psyche in the later years casts an intense light on what happens in the early years. Only an educational theory which sees the developmental process as a whole can deal adequately with any part of it.

The difficulty is in part semantic. In physical terms the growing up process goes on until the maximum growth is reached, and then it stops. The temptation is great to carry this over to education, and to see it as ending when the growing up process ends, with the college and professional school years. Thus the youth has presumably been prepared for what he will do and be after his schooling, when he has grown up. Hence the idea of "commencement"—going out into "the world" and starting "life."

John Dewey warned against this danger. In *My Pedagogic Creed,* as early as 1897, he wrote that "education is a process of living and not a preparation for future living." I should myself prefer "growing" to "living." Education is the discovery and deployment of whatever resources, in the person and his environments, are best calculated to help in his learning and growing, and in the fullest development of his possibilities. It is in itself a process of growing and experiencing in the total life span and not merely a preparation for later growing and experiencing. We won't rid ourselves of an essentially provincial approach to education until we drop the idea that it is only for the young and only a preparation for something "realer" still to come.

In this sense the seductive idea of being "grown up" is also a treacherous idea. Unlike physical growth, the growth of the personality and psyche has no terminal point except death itself. It is evolutionary in the best Darwinian sense—that it is a continuing process, not necessarily toward "higher" stages of development but certainly toward later and more complex ones. Perception, awareness, cognition, insight, intuition, creativeness—these move from phase to phase in the individual's life span. From conception, birth, and earliest infancy until the end, growing and learning are a succession of phases in the life history, a continuous process.

But not an even one. There are phases of the life history when breakthroughs occur, although we are not yet clear about just when they come, or why then. It is a little like William James' metaphor of the flights and perchings of a bird. In the individual's life history the flights come in infancy, in early childhood, in adolescence, in early manhood and womanhood, in middle life, in early old age. They come not only in response to biological changes (motor, endocrinological, sexual), but also to psychosocial changes, in the form of identity crises, relationships to family and others, and the perception of self and the world. The two periods of breakthrough that have been most intensely studied are childhood (largely because of the Freudian stress on the psychoanalytic theory of the child) and adolescence. The others would repay richly an equally concentrated study.

The controversy about whether learning comes faster and easier in the early years than the later is a fruitless one, because it varies with what is being learned. On many scores a child learns faster than an adult, and more effortlessly—in bodily skills and rhythms, in languages, in emotional growth, perhaps in leaps of intuition. Yet the creative process, which is the heart of the learning and growing experience, not only continues through middle manhood and womanhood but even into the late decades, taking subtler and more ambitious forms than the early years allowed.

Are there times in human development when the moment for learning must be seized, or the occasion is lost? I believe there are. But this is truer of skills leading to mastery or creativeness of a high order—as with mastery of multiple languages or of musical or dancing skills, or original work in mathematics—than it is of the more ordinary run of skills.

Jerome Bruner's statement, that one can teach any subject at any age with some degree of effectiveness provided one finds the right level of communication, was a healthy counterfoil to the more traditional view that there is a set sequence of subjects appropriate for a set development of faculties and skills in the learner. Yet the rub lies of course exactly in the question of finding teachers who in turn can find the right level of communication. The failures encountered with the "new mathematics," which grew out of the Bruner Committee's work in the 1960s, were failures in communication rather than in theory, but they were just as fatal. One can agree that some degree of learning can take place at any age, in any subject, with the proper teaching, and at the same time assert that what counts for the individual is readiness to learn that particular skill or insight in his own particular development. Readiness is all, but it doesn't come at the same time for all, nor on the same subjects for all.

Throughout learning and development theory the great enemy is rigidity. And one of the worst forms that rigidity takes is determinism of method—that unless some particular method or ritual is used, preferably early in childhood, the child's life will be blighted forever. Americans seem to have been characteristically pushovers for this idea of destiny in the nursery, whether under the spell of Puritanism (the child must be saved from the ways of sin), or of John B. Watson's Behaviorism (the child is a *tabula rasa,* and whatever script you write into it in its earliest infancy will condition its responses forever), or of psychoanalysis (there are fateful paths, whether of toilet training, or breast feeding, or maternal attention or inattention, or sexual stimulation, which lead to repression and neuroses or to mental health), or of educational progressivism (stay clear of discipline and punishments, minimize interventions, let the healthy instincts of the child assert themselves, or the child will come to grief), or of traditional values theory which is a carry-over from the Puritan ethos (set the child in the right path early, instill the right values, give the values the sanction of discipline and of rewards and punishment, or else the child will end delinquent or alienated or a life failure).

The fact is that none of these approaches was totally without merit. There is a kernel of validity in each. The trouble lies with making each a universal, embodying it in a dogma, clothing it with the or-else that turned it into a system of anxiety and fear. The history of parental consciousness in America has been a stations-of-the-cross progress from one to another of these agonized systems of destiny through rigid faith.

I shall be examining in the next section, on psychologies as options in the theory and arts of education, whatever some valid elements there are in each of the psychologies, provided we strip them of determinism and dogma. The historical pilgrimage of Americans through these approaches may be viewed as a sequence of experimental adventures which have left a residue on the current state of theory and art. The problem is to throw out what is harmful, save what is useful and insightful, resolve the contradictions between them, and bring them into a larger overall focus which gives each part a new meaning. It is a difficult task, but not impossible.

The total developmental story is one of polarities and dialectic. It is not true, as the Puritans thought, that the child is born with original sin, and must be purged of it. Yet it is certainly true that all of us have a double endowment, including the aggressive-destructive as well as the creative, and that both must be reckoned with. It is not true that destiny is decided in the nursery, beyond preadventure, forever and ever. Yet it is certainly true that the earlier growing years cast their shadow on the later ones, that much which happens in the earlier ones—repressions, cruelties, lack of love, overpossessiveness, symbiotic relationships with parents, failure to find identification models, failure in the internalizing of values—is reflected in anomie, lack of affect, and personality and character distortions in later years.

There is a valid function to be performed by interventions—by parents, siblings, teachers—in the earlier years, yet many interventions have proved blundering and repressive. There is an even more valid role for freedom of development, yet the wrong kind of freedom at the wrong time has led to a sense of emptiness along with a meaningless willfulness. There is a malleability in the human organism, yet the genetic factors are there, and cannot be ignored: sometimes triumphantly, sometimes tragically, the final victory belongs to them.

There is a role for habits, as William James saw, provided they don't become rigid and stultifying ones. There is a role for will, in setting habits or breaking away from old channelings and directions and opening new ones, thus carving out one's destiny, as Otto Rank insisted. There is the excitement and creativeness of freedom in the earlier developmental years, and also in the rediscovery of freedom in the later ones. But there is also the need for limit-setting, whether by parental authority or one's own will.

There is the heady excitement of being a self-starter and self-sustainer, with an autonomous relation to the imperatives of work. But there is also the well-attested role of reward and reenforcement in the learning process, and the interaction of outer approval and inner exhilaration. There is the impact of the environment on the individual—the presence, or absence, of adequate nutrition, housing, medical care, open space, school facilities. There are also the instances of the transcendence of environmental limitations, and the triumph of character, intelligence, and will over a limiting social environment.

These are the polar opposites that play out their roles in the developmental drama. Any account of that drama which omits the clash and conflict of these polar opposites, and pretends that one or the other partner in the pairs doesn't exist, does violence to the dialectical truth. The American philosopher Morris R. Cohen, who was perhaps the best exponent of the method of polarities in philosophy, showed how they operated in the two areas he knew best— science and law. It can be applied as well to education and development. There is an interaction between the polar elements, in which each changes and is changed by the other. And there is a transcendence of each, in a resolution of the opposites which becomes a synthesis. This kind of resolution and synthesis is the task both of the educational thinker and the parent or teacher, but it would be an impossible task if the potentials for resolution and synthesis were not already there in the developmental situation itself.

This is true also of the two concepts with which this section began—growing up and growing. There is some validity in the idea of focusing special attention on the years through adolescence, since the post-puberty years, the ending of physical growth, the wrestling with adolescent sexuality, the forming of close friendships, the discoveries of a career line of direction, all represent a crucial watershed in development. This is a watershed in the developmental stream. But it is also true that the process of growing continues after adolescence, that there are other watersheds to come, other copings and wrestlings with new experience, other sexual and identity crises.

The false ideas about "growing up" and growing have permeated us deeply. Thus we assume that the life pattern we reach when we have "grown up" and "settled down" is the one we are stuck with. Supposedly there are no new continents of learning and growing to conquer, no new seas to venture on. This may explain why some of the recent awareness movements, opening up new life-styles, have hit so many people in middle age so hard. Suddenly they discover that they don't have to be encased in a psychic armor, frozen until the end, but that they can start on new careers and relationships and discover new possibilities within themselves.

We are so bemused by the encrusted myth that we lose confidence. We find ourselves doing fewer things for the first time and more for the last time, and we slip into doing nothing all the time, until finally we do one thing for the first and last time—die. It doesn't have to be thus. The alternative is to be open to new experience until the end—to continue growing and learning until we grow into the unlearned, the unknown, and unknowable.

The resolution is found if we understand that each of the successive phases of the life continuum has its own conditions of learning and growing, its own vulnerabilities, its own creativeness, its own agonies of confrontation and transformation. I happen to believe—and will argue it in Chapter 4 below—that the traditional sequence of exposures in the course of the life cycle must be rethought. But what I stress here is that the total flow of the life force through all the years of our lives is the only real raw material of the educational process. This alone is primary. Everything else is imposed from without and contrived from within. Education itself is a social invention— a highly complex and ingenious one, but still an invention. We sometimes act as if the life process must be truncated in order to fit the Procrustean bed of the educational categories. A good many of our present discontents with education come exactly from that attempt.

There are two crucial facts about this life flow which we need to reckon with if we are not to move too far from the reality principle. One is that we are dealing with organisms—the learner as an organism, the teacher as an organism, the school, culture, community, and society as different kinds of organisms, but still organisms. The developmental story is enacted by and within these organisms. It is a good principle to *go with the organism* while assessing the need for various interventions and their psychic cost, and while seeking a resolution of the polarities in the developmental process that I have described.

The other fact is that the life force flowing through these organisms is exactly that—a life force. Where it comes from is a mystery we have never resolved. We make the mystery more specific, but no readier of solution, when we say that it comes from the human gene, which in turn has developed from billions of years of various life forms, and millions of years in the evolution of the human family. Being a life force, it has fluctuations within the history of each organism—a rise and fall of energy that is in part biologically determined but also in part a matter of choice and will. A good teacher—whether at home, at school, or on the job—heightens the energy field around him and makes the life force in everyone flow more strongly. Beyond biological limits, beyond the determinism of operant or aversive conditioning, the learning process is affected by the ebb and flow of the life force in the interacting organisms.

Being a life force in a mortal organism, its fire must at some point die down and finally be extinguished. But until that time, as long as the fire and the flow are there, the learning and growing process continues, taking resourceful new forms, and compensating for the running down of sheer physical energy by an imaginative energy and by the distillation of experience which we call ripeness and wisdom.

A third fact, to add to the two I have mentioned, and flowing from them: The onrush of experience, each episode with its confrontation of opposites, is the matrix out of which comes the flow of value formation. The theorists sometimes speak of values as if they came full-blown out of nothing and nowhere. They come out of the millions of years of experience in the primitive and modern societies which have formed the human family.

The individual teacher and student don't start from scratch. They are the inheritors of this long stretch of years that have preceded them in the course of human history. They carry within them the force and potential of the gene, the flow of the life force. But they carry within them also a value-creating need which is, quite simply, the need to give meaning to their experience, and the need to arm themselves for coping with the experience to come.

Thus the essence of the developmental story is more than growing up, and more even than continuing to grow. It is more than what we call education. It takes Dewey's concept of experience and education and reaches both before experience—to the human organism and the life flow from which experience derives— and also beyond experience—to the meanings which humans give to their experience, the meanings they hack out like a path through the undergrowth of their experience.

It also reaches beyond education, for education is only one aspect—although a central one—of the total meaningful life force. It is nothing if it is not a values-shaping and values-defining instrument. But the values it shapes and defines don't start with the school or even the family. They are present in the phylogenetic experience of the human race which expresses itself in diverse ways in the history of the society and the family, and in the ontogeny of the life history of the particular individual.

Amidst the welter of experience in the individual life, within the context of community and society, the choice between competing, conflicting, and confused values is a hard one, but it is a matter of life and death. Education must help in that process of choice. Which is what makes education, as I have suggested, a life-and-death matter, and therefore the most perilous of adventures.

The Unbroken Web

Educational theory today is crucially psychology-oriented. It was not always thus. In Europe and early America it was oriented toward religious care and toward the schoolmaster's art as a species of it. Later it was oriented toward fashioning a gentleman who would be concerned with politics, law, his estates, philosophic and scientific speculation, and the arts of living. For the lower orders it was oriented toward the useful arts. In the eighteenth century it was oriented toward moral philosophy.

The orientation toward psychology as a special form of moral philosophy came late in the eighteenth and early in the nineteenth centuries, along with the orientation toward the novel in Europe, and the emergence of the middle classes in Europe and America as the prime force in a democracy. I see Rousseau's *Emile* as the central symbolic event linking all three— the middle classes, fiction (or drama, later the media), and the exploration of psychology. I speak of the novel because in its day it served the purpose that the magazines, TV, and the film serve today—that of teaching life-styles and philosophies by example. It was a kind of ambulatory psychology. Its great practitioners were better psychologists, and therefore better educators, than the psychologists and educators themselves. It all amounted to an effort by the middle class, in cherishing its children, to find ways of molding them and setting them on the right path, without a lead from the tumbling and vanishing aristocracies.

In essence this meant viewing education as the prime theory and art of character formation. This has been, in fact, its longest and most continuous tradition. Psychology should have been the ideal discipline toward this end in the family, the schoolroom, or wherever. But something curious happened to educational psychology on its way toward this role. It separated itself from moral philosophy, very much the way politics and economics did. Narcissus-like, it fell in love with its own reflection in the mirror of science and forgot that its obligations were not to some concept of science but to the theory and arts of the growth of personality and the shaping of mind and character.

The fact is, of course, that there can be no psychology of education in a vacuum, any more than there can be a psychology of politics or economics or law or religion in a vacuum. The psychologies that are applied to education must be psychologies which can also shed light on every other phase of human behavior and conduct. That is to say, they must be whole in themselves, as behaviorism is, or psychoanalysis, or Gestalt, or human potential psychology. The seeming exceptions are the cognitive or structural school, which has focused on learning theory, and the related developmental school whose adherents have mostly dealt with child development. Yet the exceptions are more apparent than real, since in both cases the psychology—if it is to be valid—must apply beyond childhood to the whole life history and beyond learning to the whole life experience. It is also true that psychology, much as it has to stand by itself, never can do so completely. It is part of the intellectual experience of its time—in the sciences, social sciences, arts, philosophy. This in turn is part of the society itself, in its changes and chances.

One may call this the unbroken web that weaves together theory and practice, social thought and social action, tradition and revolution, and renewal in the society. Thus it is interesting that each of the outbursts of intellectual and social energy in America to which the term Renascence might be applied carried with it a period of vitality in educational theory and reform. This was true of the Jeffersonian period, as it was true in the period of the Renascence of the 1830s to 1850s, extending from New England and New York to the Middle West. It was true of the period of Progressivism at the turn of the twentieth century. The first of these was part of the Enlightenment, and its educational theory and reform were also part of it. The second was part of the Romantic and Transcendental movement of thought, and showed itself in the educational theory and practice of a romantic nationalism. The third was part of the movement of a new social realism, influenced heavily by both evolutionary and revolutionary thought, but also by a strong streak at once of American egalitarian and pragmatic theory. It found expression in Charles Peirce, William James, and John Dewey. Whether there will be a fourth, a half century after James and Dewey, as they in turn came a half century after Emerson, Alcott, and Horace Mann, is still unclear.

There is no exact periodicity in these waves of creative renewal. In the past the creative outbursts have come from a convergence of the sense of crisis in society and of a breakthrough in social thought. Each time they have led to another phase in the unfulfilled revolution of the educational arts. The sense of crisis is certainly true of our own time. The breakthrough in thought is yet to come. Sometimes a sense of crisis is releasing, sometimes it is merely paralyzing. The latter seems right now to apply. As for the reform in the educational arts, there is considerable fanfare, but even more conflict and confusion. It should be obvious enough that the impetus of the revolutions of the 1960s has largely spent itself. Everything depends now upon affecting a synthesis between innovation in educational method and clarity of educational thought. If the ground can be seeded in the decade to come, and the young shoots carefully tended, the flowering should be memorable well before the end of the century.

The James-Dewey Watershed

Central to the clarification process is the effort to find among the competing psychological schools an available psychology which will serve as an all-purpose guide for everyone involved in education. This is of course an impossible assignment, yet it is one that teachers have come to insist on.

The closest they came to achieving it was with William James and John Dewey during the first quarter of the century. Looking back at it, one gets the feeling of a flawed idyll. The conditions seemed rife for a great leap forward in education. Schools and teachers were multiplying. With the Populist revolt and the Wilsonian progressivism, reform was in the air. In the universities—and outside—there was a burst of new thought. From across the sea—especially from Germany—there were reports of a new science of psychology emerging, laboratory-based, largely experimental, with Wilhelm Wundt as one of its great figures. William James, like many other Americans, had gone to Germany to study, had chosen medicine over philosophy, had run into a nervous breakdown, and had returned to America to offer courses at Harvard on physiology and psychology. Young John Dewey, who had written in Michigan about Leibnitz, but also about his pedagogical creed, was to come to Chicago and open an experimental laboratory school, combining aspects about the seamless web of thought and action from the "pragmatism" of Charles Peirce and William James into his own phrase, "learning by doing." James published a book of principles of psychology, based on his Harvard course, and carried the gospel of the new discipline to teachers groups around the nation, in his *Talks to Teachers.* Dewey was trying not only to fashion a new educational credo for a democracy but also to apply the democratic credo to education. There was a sense of exhilaration in teaching and thinking in such a dawn.

The spectacle of two great American philosophers— one of them the father of American psychology—talking to teachers about their common concerns in language as old as the oldest philosophy and as young as the newest psychology has no parallel today. One reason they were able to talk to teachers was because philosophy and psychology had not yet become separated. James was telling them about consciousness as a flowing stream; Dewey described both democracy and education in terms of process. In both cases there was a feeling of dynamism, innovation, relevance.

Why then do I speak of it as a flawed idyll? The flaw lay exactly where the strength should have been. I have said that philosophy and psychology had not yet broken away from each other. But they had lost their connection with the kind of common social theory they had in the moral philosophy of Hobbes, Locke, Rousseau, and Burke. They have never regained it. With an increasingly difficult society—more alienated, less cohesive, less governable—a social theory embedded within a larger philosophy, carrying with it a psychology, an ethic, and a sense of the mythic and the sacral, has become not a luxury but a necessity. It was the fateful lack of such a social theory in the first two great decades of the century that flawed and doomed the important work of James and Dewey.

William James' strength lay in his undogmatic sense of possibility, both in society and in thought. He had a febrile eagerness for new insights and an openness to experience. He was against any sort of closure as he was against any form of absolutism in thought. In fact, his only absolute lay in his anti-absolutism and his antimonism. Confronted by the need to define his universe, he denied that there was one and saw instead a multiverse. The second volume of his *Psychology* was organized around the traditional categories of habit, memory, will, and the rest, yet he was open to the possibility of a psychic pluriverse, studied mysticism, conversion, and the whole range and variety of religious experience, and was in fact the father—at least in America—of what we have come to call the "transpersonal" psychology of a separate reality.

His weakness was a correlate of his strength. He saw multiplicity, but couldn't envisage the unity within which it was enclosed—saw the many, but not the many within the one. His openness to experience in his pragmatism trembled on the brink of accepting the dominant experience of his time—because it was dominant, as well as because it was experience. In the end he held back, but others who followed him didn't have his fine restraint and tumbled over the brink in what Lewis Mumford was to call "the pragmatic acquiescence." James himself was aware of the dangers of acquiescing in the values of his day, as witness his searing phrase about "the Bitch-Goddess, Success." He understood the anomie of the "gilded youth" of his time and their need for struggle, aggressiveness, and heroism. Yet the "moral alternative to war" which he recommended—a kind of Civilian Conservation Corps—proved too marginal to resolve the problem of man's double endowment. The fact was that neither James nor any of his contemporaries—nor any American thinker since—has effectively tussled with the difficulties of constructing what Walter Lippmann (a disciple of James and later of Graham Wallas) was to call a "public philosophy"— something in a modern democracy to take the place of the ancient Chinese "mandate of Heaven." In fact, he would shrink from the very thought that such a unifying, cohesive theory of man, history, and society was either possible or desirable. The irony was that one of the rare examples among American thinkers of a whole man left a vacuum at the most crucial point in his thought, where there should have been wholeness.

I have written of John Dewey at some length elsewhere, and will limit myself here to his bearing on the theme of the search for an adequate social theory. Dewey was less creative than James in psychology, less prescient about the needs that later generations were to discover, less in touch with his unconscious and therefore with that of others, less crisp and incandescent as a stylist in language and ideas. But he was more systematic, better acquainted with the great traditional problems of a technical philosophy, and more exacting in fitting educational theory into his larger philosophical frame. That was why much of Dewey's thinking—virtues, weaknesses, and all— moved into the vacuum that James left.

It proved the wrong peg in the wrong hole. Its intent was all to the good. As with Horace Mann some 75 years earlier, Dewey's time was faced with a new (and later) industrialism, a new economic elite, a new class system, an even more massive influx of waves of immigration that had to be absorbed and integrated into the society, and therefore with a more acute phase of the problems of cohesion, estrangement, atomism, anomie. The larger answer he gave was in the form of a philosophical system which included a politics, economics, aesthetic, ethic, metaphysic, and even religion (*A Common Faith*). The crucial ingredients of the philosophy were nature, experience, experiment, process, change. What finally emerged from this was a theory of a restated liberal democracy permeating every phase of social experience, with the emphasis on state intervention in the economic process but on individual choice in all other areas, and indeed on the primacy of felt needs and actions over continuity, tradition, and institutionalized value choices.

Dewey's system building was by no means dogmatic.

His system was open enough for many options to
be drawn from it. But the impetus from the whole
surrounding envelope of ideas in the intellectual
Renascence of the turn of the century—from Beard
and Robinson in history, from Pound in law, from
Veblen and Commons in economics, from Smith and
Beard in political theory, from the Populists and the
Progressives, from the muckrakers like Lincoln Stef-
fens, from Boas in anthropology, from Parrington in
the history of literature, from Hemingway and Dos
Passos in the novel, from John Reed and Max Eastman
in the mystique of revolution—was an impetus toward
radical change. Dewey's experimentalism and democracy in education could conceivably have contained
this impetus, but actually fed it. His disciples were
many, but few were conservatives or even moderates.
There seemed no attraction in his philosophy for those
who sought continuities, either in history or life.

It might be argued with some credibility that, given
the Marxist trends in the world after 1917, Dewey's
philosophy kept a strong Marxism from developing
in American education, and equally that amidst the
irrationalisms set in motion by the Freudian revolution, Dewey's emphasis on the method of reason kept
American education for a long period from some of
the irrationalisms that have beset it more recently.
But it remains true that one of Dewey's disciples,
Sidney Hook, saw in Dewey's pragmatism a link with
Marxist humanism, and that another of his disciples,
George Counts, picked up the radical overtones of
possibility in Dewey's philosophy and called on the
schools to "build a new social order."

Neither of these came to pass. They both proved
feckless. But the movement of "progressivism" in
education did come to pass. Lawrence Cremin has
dealt with it, in sweeping perspective and meticulous
detail, in his *Transformation of the American School.*
I can only add, without putting the responsibility on
him for my heresies, that while the movement followed

from the logic of its time as well as from Dewey's own logic, it came too soon with too much. Too soon because it had no psychology, no social theory, no values theory, no metaphysic, no public philosophy, except those of a vaguely radical liberalism. It would have come better if it had waited and helped those to develop as a frame for educational reform. I say it also came with too much, because it brought with it a cloudburst of hopes, and a proliferation of new educational methods which were largely abstracted both from the social realities of the evolving class and ethnic system and from the needs of survival of the American civilization in an increasingly hostile global environment, with increasingly centrifugal forces operating from within, when cohesion and continuity rather than a plethora of atomistic freedoms would prove to be the real need.

I recognize that this is largely historic twenty-twenty hindsight, yet what else do we have in assessing the long range validity of ideas except their consequences as they worked themselves out through the flux and logic of history? I once wrote that "Ideas are weapons." Paul Weaver, on the conservative side of our battlefield, wrote that "ideas have consequences." These were different aspects of the same basic vision—that what counts in fashioning the destinies of a society lies in the realm of the imagination as much as anywhere else, that we project our dreams and needs and wishes in the form of the ideas we shape and follow, and that they are to be judged not only by how effective they are in battle but by what happens to them after the contemporary battles are over. Dewey's ideas were effective in battle for a time, but they didn't remain in possession of the battlefield. What followed was a handful of dust and a desolate emptiness where there should have been a continuing and changing meaning.

Where the progressive education movement ran into the greatest difficulty was with the lower-middle class, whose sense of traditional values it outraged with its permissiveness, and also with the blacks, whose need was for greater freedom and the chance for expressiveness. It also ran into trouble with the more tough-minded elements in American life, especially in business, politics, the military, and the professions. This reached its climax during the Sputnik panic in American educational circles. This crisis, coming as late as it did, simply hammered the nails tighter in the coffin that had already enclosed the movement. What is doubly ironic here was that a movement coming out of the "tough-minded" pragmatism of James and Dewey should have become (the phrases are James') as "tender-minded" as it did. Its vagueness, its flight from discipline and form, its appeal to feminine rather than masculine values, led to its not being taken with any deep seriousness by either the power elite or the new intellectual elites. Actually it offered little room for elite theory and seemed hostile to it. Not wholly by accident it coincided with the dominance of women in the teaching posts and the feminine watch that was placed over the strategic passes of value formation.

If I seem too harshly to bid farewell to the most promising period in the history of American education it is because I am saying farewell to part of my own time and my own past, and because history itself said farewell to it. As I shall develop the theme in the next chapter, there were a number of assassins responsible for the demise of the great hopes attached to the educational system. I have addressed myself here to only one because it was the most closely associated with educational theory and with the intellectual breakthrough of the first third of the century.

Neither the forties nor the fifties offered much to replace it. The sixties brought with them strong political activisms which fed into a renewal of largely Marxist ideas and programs for education, and an equally strong counter-culture which fed into the triad of human potential psychology, the growth-center and awareness movements, and the transpersonal movements and psychologies. I shall be dealing with all of them in the chapters that follow. But it is notable that after the James-Dewey watershed came the rains and floods which somehow did little for the parched earth.

Six Schools in Search of a Workable Psychology

After the flawed dream of progressivist reform there was for a time a queasiness about educational philosophies and utopian movements. The field was left largely to the psychologists, who could fashion and sell their intellectual wares without a commitment beyond their own discipline. It was more secure that way. Besides, there may have been the unspoken hope that if education could find an adequate psychology the rest would follow.

There is no wholly accurate or just way to present the doctrines of the competing psychologies, or even to select them without doing violence to their own lack of definition and their overlappings. My choice of six of them is at best arbitrary, but it will serve as a starting point for the reader who has his own array. My six are: *Behaviorism, Gestalt psychology, psychoanalytic and psychotherapy systems, cognitive and developmental psychologies, human potential psychology,* and the *transpersonal psychologies.* I shall try, as with James and Dewey, to present both their strengths and vulnerabilities, and—where possible—their relation to social structures. If I seem to caricature any or all of them, I ask the reader to assign it not to my intent but to the summary nature of the task I pose. I might add that my intent is less to brush them aside than it is to show what resources of psychological thinking are available today for educational thought and practice, and what kind of workable synthesis can be made of them.

What is best about behaviorism is its sharpness and tough-mindedness, as befits a psychology which is at once mechanistic (stimulus-response-reenforce-

ment) and determinist. There are few blurred edges
and little softness about behaviorist therapy and behavior modification. The psychologist-as-observer also
becomes the psychologist-as-manipulator. He sets up
the environment; he organizes the conditioning,
whether "operant" or "aversive;" he doses out the
"reenforcement" in order to get the desired modification of behavior. Teaching thus becomes the ultimate
in acting upon the student, and learning becomes the
ultimate in his being acted upon.

Behaviorism   bypasses   the   whole   authority-
obedience issue in the teacher-student relation by
assuming the authority of the teacher and programming
the obedience of the student. Its learning theory
becomes one of classifying good and bad learning
habits, and using rewards and punishments to set them
right, re-enforcing the desirable ones, deterring the
undesirable ones.

In the broader area, outside the classroom, it undercuts the problem of political belief and political
religion by programing the desired beliefs, thus re-
moving both the options and the mystique from both
revolutionary and conservative political credos. Its
model for the human being is that of a computer rather
than of an organism. Its utopia would thus be that
of a myriad of computerized individuals within a larger
computerized society. Its stress is on what these
isolated entities have in common rather than on what
differentiates them or on what is the connective tissue
between them. It maximizes the calculable and mini-
mizes the incalculable. It finds irrelevant all values
(witness the Skinnerian "beyond freedom and dignity") except those it can program and control and
get a feedback from. Its values are not the questions
put to life but the questions put to the individual
as a mechanism. These values are not internalized
but memorized—that is, stored in the memory banks,
to be retrieved under the proper stimulus as in Burgess'
Clockwork Orange. In that sense, behaviorism elimi-

nates education as either self-discovery or self-discipline by eliminating the major part of freedom of choice. It substitutes conditioning for prediction, since prediction is either a tautology or meaningless unless there are variables along with regularities of behavior.

From Pavlov and Watson, through Hull, to Skinner, this has been the pathway of behaviorism. It has many things going for its effectiveness. It has fitted in with the needs of the industrial technology, of advertising and public relations, and of military training, since it makes people more manageable as counters for conditioning and manipulation. For the same reason it has been impressively effective in therapy: it achieves results by changing the undesirable behavior patterns, even though it doesn't get at their sources in past experience. Whether this bypassing of causes in order to achieve desired results will mean a stored-up psychic cost in the end isn't yet clear. One might argue in response that this is a psychic parallel to the bypass technique in heart surgery, and that both are justified by their results, and that the clever tactics are as admissible in the human organism as in military struggle or in what Kant called the "ruses of history."

A second school, whose boundaries are not yet clear, one may call *cognitive-developmental*. Its leaders are Jean Piaget in Europe and—despite some differences from Piaget—Jerome Bruner in America. More recently *developmental psychology* has burst the bounds of the cognitive, has made a number of recruits among the therapy schools, and may well become a full-fledged psychological school in its own right. (I shall be dealing later with the applications of the psychoanalytical schools themselves to childhood in the work of Anna Freud, Melanie Klein, and their American variants, including Erik Erikson's work.)

Piaget's thinking is more severely rational than is true of the others. What fascinates him is how the mind of the child unfolds as it moves toward abstractions and conceptual capacity. Bruner may have a point when he guesses that Piaget is more concerned with epistemology—the theory of knowledge itself—than with the psychology of childhood. His own work goes beyond Piaget in moving toward a synthesis of the cognitive and intuitive and making allowance also for different structural relationships among nonwhite ethnic groups in non-Western societies. This may point the way for a new direction toward a *structural psychology*, with a triangular relationship between the child's *psyche*, the nature of the learning problem, and the nature and traditions of the society. This would bring it closer also toward the structural anthropology of Claude Levi-Strauss, whose impact on European thought and literature has been an important one but has not yet reached American educational theory. In overall terms the weakness of the cognitive-developmental psychology lies in its almost exclusive concern with the childhood years and with learning theory, its lesser concern with a therapeutic approach, its failure (except in the work of Erikson) to incorporate a theory of society, and its minimal concern with values and value formation.

With the *Gestalt* school, whether in the seminal work of Wertheimer, Koffka, Goldstein, or Lewin, the narrow selective environment of behaviorism is broadened into a total figure-ground pattern, with the focus on the interaction between the parts and the whole. This avoids both the mechanistic and manipulative aspects of behaviorism, as it avoids also the dualism of the reasoning and intuitive faculties. The strength of *Gestalt* lies exactly in its refusal to peel away any aspect of human behavior from the whole of it. Along with the humanistic school, which I shall be discussing, it can make the best claim for offering a *holistic* approach to the total personality. In the work of Kurt Goldstein, notably in *The Organism*, the holistic and organismic are combined with the basic *Gestalt* aspects to form an impressive approach which foreshadows the humanistic school while exerting a tighter discipline over its material. It is not generally noted how much Abraham Maslow borrowed from Kurt Goldstein in shaping his own theory. Curiously *Gestalt* has not rooted itself deeply in the American intellectual landscape, perhaps because its great figures were emigres from the Weimar Republic who carried over from Germany their strict experimental discipline and their anti-Freudian hostility but who could not find recruits in America as the psychoanalytic emigres did. The American soil is fertile for therapies, less so for the scrupulous work (in perception theory and related fields) of scholars who have been unable to generalize their approach to cover America's deep concerns.

The most familiar and controversial psychology, along with behaviorism, is found in the *psychotherapeutic* schools. I call them that, rather than Freudian or psychoanalytic, because there are neo-Freudian, post-Freudian, and nonanalytically oriented schools as well. In fact, the proliferation of sub-schools in addition to the more orthodox Freudian one—Jungian, Adlerian, Rankian, Left Freudian, Sullivanian, Horneyan, ego-analytical (Hartman, Kris, and others), Eriksonian, Existentialist (Binswanger, May, Frankel) and many others—is one of the striking facts about this cluster of schools.

It argues two things in the main—the fertile ground that American life and thought offer to these brands of theory, and their own infinite vitality and adaptability. The American, as the archetypal man of the West, has become therapeutic man—healer and to be healed. Inevitably the mounting figures on mental illness find expression in the classroom, just as they cripple the growth process in the postschooling years. Inevitably also the intellectual climate dominated by the therapeutic approach gets reflected in the learning experience, on the assumption that blockages and resistances to learning are the very Devil and must be exorcised by the teacher-therapist. I have to add that the resistances and blockages to growth on the teacher's side are less often recognized: the physician doesn't always know how to medicine himself.

Unlike most schools of psychology, which start as descriptions of reality and move from there to therapy, the psychotherapy schools reverse the process. They start as strategies for therapy and then move to a description of reality. The result is that this cluster of psychologies has become more sickness-oriented than is healthy either for the practitioners or their body of doctrine. On the score of determinism the usual criticism of this school—that it allows little scope for the free-functioning individual will—must now be amended, since a number of the therapies (ego psychology, will therapy, existential psychology) stress the assertion of consciousness (will), and belief as part of the therapy. This is true also of the criticism that these psychologies are too past-oriented and don't deal adequately with the individual's resources in the present and future. It is this capacity to adapt themselves to shifting currents of thought and criticism which forms one of the strengths of these psychologies.

Other strengths can be cited—the insight into the unconscious, the recognition of the force of repression, the stress on the instinctual, indeed of the daemonic, the effort to deal with the life-and-death phases of the psyche. It is in these areas that the dark roots of both creativeness and destructiveness are to be sought. If the school can rid itself of much of its jargon, overcome the rigidities of some of its practitioners, and move toward a health orientation instead of a sickness orientation, it will remain a viable approach in every phase of education.

It is harder to predict the viability of human potential or *humanistic psychology*. It first emerged, in the work of Abraham Maslow, Carl Rogers, and others, as a revolt against the determinisms of both psychoanalysis and behaviorism, calling itself for a time the *Third Force* psychology. It was also a response to the wide-

spread feeling that a psychology was needed to express
the free as against the conditioned, the healthy as
against the abnormal. Yet it is still too much of a
grab bag of bits and pieces from other schools and
from the reactions against them. If it has a unity it
is in the central approach of seeing the person as
a subject, not an object—as basically malleable, with
an inner drive toward health, creativeness, and fulfillment. It is therefore strongly oriented toward learning
and growth at every stage of the life cycle.

Of all the schools I have discussed, humanistic
psychology is hardest to define. The reason may be
that it is less a psychological discipline than an attitude
toward psychology and toward the fulfillment of
human potentials. Hence the blurring of its outlines,
the glow of humanism and hope that suffuses it, and
its lack of a sharply defined vocabulary and set of
technical concepts. (By the same token it avoids much
of the gibberish that has come to afflict all the other
schools I have discussed, especially the psychotherapies and the cognitive school.) It attracts political
liberals to its cause, where psychologies like behaviorism attract conservatives. One might call it—and even
more the transpersonal school which is an offshoot
of it—a *soft* psychology where the others are *hard*
psychologies. There is an irony in this, especially since
William James, to whom both schools owe much, was
the first to contrast tender-minded and tough-minded
thinking and clearly opt for the latter. As compared
with the schools deriving from Freud and his circle,
against whom the psychological humanists have broken many a lance, the humanists take too little account
of the instinctual (although they build heavily on the
premise of repression) and of death and the darkly
daemonic in the human endowment. I recall a workshop at Esalen with a brilliant humanistic psychologist
who eagerly awaited the age ahead when man would
no longer have any vestige of the tragic in life. I
couldn't help exclaiming, "Don't take my night away!"

This strongly optimist bent is crucial to the school
and accounts in part for its appeal in a time of darkness.
It makes the humanist psychology a natural among
educators who deal with the poor and the socially
disadvantaged and gives it an impact among social
case workers, welfare workers, and prison reformers.
It thus shares the basic premise of most liberals—that
those who are in a mess owe it to their social environment, which has stunted their psychic growth. Even
the family history, whether with parents and siblings
or with mates, is viewed as another form of environment. The remedy is to explore new depths of consciousness and awareness, to change the outer environment by changing the life-style, and the inner
environment by getting a more accepting sense of self
and a more embracing attitude toward others, and thus
to release the potential for growth which has all along
been there, like an imprisoned maiden, waiting for
her savior prince.

There is power in this approach as a reaction against
the dour view that the imprisoned maiden must remain
imprisoned, either until she confesses her trans-
gressions or until some deliverer shrink guides her
all the way back, by an Ariadne thread, into the dark
fortress where her Minotaur father first crushed her
spirit. The true strength of the humanist school lies
in the affirmation of the positive, healthy energies
in the human endowment, which are shared in varying
degrees by all members of the human family. In this
respect the school reawakens echoes of the great
Utopians in Europe of the seventeenth and eighteenth
centuries and marks an effort to launch a new Enlightenment in America, picking up where Jefferson left
off with his "pursuit of happiness" and his belief
in the people.

Curiously the humanists share one major assumption
with their enemies, the behaviorists—that, along with
our innate individual strength, we are environmentally
conditioned and can be changed by a change in the
environmental conditioning. The crucial difference

lies in defining the environment and also the agent of change. For the behaviorists the environment is a narrow one—a laboratory or quasi-laboratory—and the agents of change are the small elite who program the changed conditioning. For the humanists the environment is the total life-style, and the agents of change are the individuals themselves, working either alone or with their functional group in some form of communal quarters, in a therapy or meditation group, or at a growth center.

The history of humanistic psychology runs parallel to the history of growth-centers and communes, which may be seen roughly as their experimental laboratories. Thus the school came in a sense out of the development of the counter-culture, from the late fifties through the sixties and into the mid-seventies. One influence on it came from the Orient, finding expression at the start of the sixties in the Esalen Center, under Michael Murphy and Richard Price who brought Aldous Huxley, Gerald Heard, Abraham Maslow, Carl Rogers, and Fritz Perls to their workshop. Out of Esalen the whole growth center movement radiated, moving in many directions—open sexuality, open marriage, nudism, confluent education, George Leonard's vision of ecstasy in the classroom, TA (Transactional Analysis), TM (Transcendental Meditation), Arica, sensory awareness and training, deep massage, release of bodily rigidities.

Another influence came from Maslow's work in motivation theory, the holistic emphasis (largely shaped by Kurt Goldstein's organismic thinking), his stress on "peak experiences" and on hierarchies of needs and values, and in general his strong affirmations combined with a good sense of timing in the history of psychology. A third strong influence came from a number of people involved in therapy as Maslow had not been, notably Carl Rogers, Rollo May, and others, who were discontented with the instrumentalist attitude of the Freudian and post-Freudian schools, and who felt that the therapeutic relationship was a partnership in the release of will, love, energy, and creativeness. It is worth noting that the Gestalt therapy of Fritz Perls, which made considerable noise for a time, had no real connections with the Gestalt school as I have discussed it, but was part of the Encounter phase of humanistic psychology and owed a good deal to dream analysis, psychodrama (the "hot seat"), and Perls' own charismatic energy.

I come finally to *transpersonal* (or psi-factor) psychology, which became fused with the counter-culture as did the humanistic school and might claim an affinity with that school. Its stress is not so much on interpersonal relationships as on the transpersonal—what goes beyond the world of the senses, of time and of space, forming (in Castaneda's phrase) a "separate reality." Thus by definition it belongs in the nonrational realm, going back to the premodern world of magic and myth, astrology, and sorcery, which fascinated Jung as it did also William James. Its motto could well be the lines from *Hamlet:* "There are more things in heaven and earth, Horatio, / Than are dreamt of in your philosophy."

Be it noted that, in the sense of tapping an unknown and unexplainable source of energy, there is an element of the transpersonal in the psychotherapies, and the humanistic disciplines, and even in behaviorism. The Extra Sensory Perception work (ESP) of J. B. Rhine was an effort to give it some laboratory verification. It has been called *parapsychology* in order to differentiate it from the accepted schools. Yet like them it deals with the psyche: in fact, it emphasizes the powers of mind over the world of the senses, through biofeedback, control of the autonomous nervous system, psychokinesis, communication with the dead and the spirit world through a medium, faith healing, and entering into a higher consciousness related to the godlike in man and to man's future transformation. Much of this comes from Eastern religion and philosophy, some of it from the experience of the Indian tradition in the Southwest, some is psychedelic and drug-induced, and a good deal of it—as with William James' *Varieties of Religious Experience*—is home grown, especially in California, which marks a new American frontier.

Clearly there is a relationship between all six of these schools and the intellectual climate, the power systems and the belief systems of modern societies. These are not bloodless battles of the categories: some of the psychologies have stirred up violent emotional responses. B. F. Skinner reported that he was greeted by an audience of 6,000 at the University of Minnesota, even while he was being hanged in effigy at Indiana University. Behaviorism has had deep American roots and has a greater current academic acceptance than any other school, yet its practical movement—Behavior Modification—arouses widespread fears. In a public discussion I once asked Skinner about these dangers. He was candid about recognizing them. But he insisted that we are already subject to conditionings in our society. We reenforce behavior on food, on sex, on aggressiveness. We are conditioned to violence by our media, even while our classrooms and homes plead against it. The contingencies of reenforcement are all slipping, he said. The immediate gratifications are invading the long range purpose of the society. The final question about a society, he said, quoting from his book, *Walden II*, is: Will it last? If America is to last, he saw no alternative except to achieve a balance between what the individual will be permitted to do for instant gratification, and what he will be conditioned to do for the sake of the future. I asked the inevitable question about his conditioning agents, *quis custodiet custodes?* Who will watch the watchmen? Who are his Platonic Guardians, and who will guard the Guardians? His answer was that we already have power elites, but that he hopes for an evolutionary selection, among the young, of those who will best be able to

move into the future by translating the healthy values
of the culture into new conditionings.

It is the most abruptly challenging theory of education—for that is what Behavior Modification amounts
to—in American educational history. In effect it repre-
sents value theory as national destiny, achieved
through a technology of the psyche. Understandably
the Soviet leaders are enthusiastic about Behavior
Modification, and in their own way practice it. The
Chinese do it more indirectly by group pressures.
Skinner is not disturbed by the totalitarian parallel.
He believes that the Soviet and American systems are
converging with each other. My own feeling is that,
even on Skinner's premise about a civilization lasting,
an educational theory of human possibility makes a
society more viable, with a freer and stronger flow
of energies, and greater innovativeness, than one of
conditioning and reenforcement.

Unlike their attitude toward behaviorism, the Soviet
leaders are strongly opposed to psychoanalysis and
the psychotherapies. In fact, they seem opposed to
all the depth psychologies, doubtless because the dark
recesses of the human psyche seem linked with political reactions and draw off energies from the positive
collective tasks. One can understand therefore why
they regard opponents of the regime as mentally sick.
On the other hand they apply themselves energetically
to some of the transpersonal techniques, since the mind
power that is generated—in psychokinesis and other
forms—can help the regime in its struggles.

Americans are on the whole not as aware of the
social implications of their psychologies. Psychoanalysis has been accepted, the psychotherapies have
spread into the school systems as elsewhere, the growth
centers have achieved a following, new life-styles are
discussed everywhere in the media, and even the
mysteries and mysticisms of the transpersonal engage
a large segment of the young, many among them
teachers. In fact, the luxuriant growth of schools and

subschools, and the emergence of the guru and the magus, in many bewildering forms, suggests a vitality in the culture which belies the predictions of civilizational doom. Some commentators believe this is a sign of decadence, and it may be. But it may equally be read as a stir of excitement, almost primitive in the way it touches myth and magic, which has in the past shown itself in the early American settlements and on the frontiers, and is a sign that the sophistication of cultural aging has not yet set in.

There are two areas, in addition to Behavior Modification, where the psychological schools have stirred up strong community controversy. One comes out of the cognitive-developmental school, which developed the IQ tests that engage ethnic passions today, and to which I shall be turning in the next chapter. The other comes out of both the humanistic and transpersonal schools and out of the counter-culture with which they interacted. It takes the form of a resistance, in Heartland America, to the challenger value system associated with these movements, which are regarded as a threat not only to the traditional values, including the religious, but to the school system itself. I shall be turning to that also in the chapter that follows.

There is a temptation, after such a review of the schools of psychology, to suggest the one right school of one's own. I shall resist it. Yet an overview of them may clarify what is more and less valid in them if one were to seek a synthesis for an educational psychology.

1) Such a psychology must be *developmental*, which is to say that it must give some account of the human life story. This is best served by the cognitive-developmental, the psychotherapies, and the humanistic school.

2) Without restricting itself to childhood it must *deal with the child*, who remains the chief preoccupation of the school system—with his cognitive development, his emotional development, his capacity to learn.

Again the three schools above serve best here.

3) It must provide an approach for *coping with classroom and schoolyard discipline, with student disaffections and student leadership.* It must also, in a related area, provide some mode of *student counselling and therapy.* Here the behavioral, psychotherapeutic, and humanistic schools serve best.

4) It must be *experimental,* either in the laboratory or classroom or in the therapy relationship. To some degree this applies to all the schools.

5) It must be *organismic,* seeing student and teacher, classroom and school system, not as mechanisms but as living organisms. Here the Gestalt and humanistic schools serve best, but none has yet evolved an adequate organismic approach.

6) It must shed a strong light on the *theory and art of instruction, learning, and communication.* Each of the schools does this, with the possible exception of the transpersonal. The strongest leads have come from the cognitive-developmental school.

7) It must be *holistic,* going beyond behavior, conduct learning, beyond cognition and intuition, beyond norms and the abnormal, to the total person and psyche and the total learning situation. This is true of Gestalt and of humanistic psychology, but even in their cases, inadequately.

8) It must deal with the *symbolic and mythical* in learning and in living, with *the realm of dreams and the imagination,* as well as with the more worldly "reality principle." Here the humanistic and transpersonal schools are of greatest service.

9) It must include a theory of *the nature of the creative process* and the dynamics of the creative leap in the teaching-learning relationship. Here all the schools have something to contribute, especially Gestalt, psychotherapeutic, and humanistic.

10) It must furnish *a theory of the society* within which education takes place—its institutions, its cul-

ture, its dynamics of change and modes of continuity, its cement of cohesiveness. Within this frame it must include a theory of the *aims of education* in striking a balance between the fulfillment of the individual and the survival of the society.

3

The Heavenly and Earthly Cities
of Education

Who Killed Our Eden? The Discontents with the School System

Since the late 1950s America has gone through a period of the shaking of the foundations. Protest, confrontation, the intense scrutiny of every institution of American life—all these started with education, on college campuses and in high school corridors, and there is little likelihood that education will cease to be a target in the future. Americans approach their perception of the good life, both of its promise and its betrayal, through the question of what happens to the career and life chances of their children. They see schooling as one of the inalienable rights set down in the Declaration and built into the promise of American life.

Since so much of America's history has been a quest of the Heavenly City through education, many of the attacks on the public schools today take on a theological character. We accuse one enemy after another of corrupting or capturing our Eden. From the earliest days of the Mathers in Massachusetts Bay to the most recent writings of Ivan Illich and the New Left, this search for the Heavenly City has implied also a hunting down of the devils who threaten it. If the early divines were certain that the schools must minister to the fear and glory of God and drive the sinful impulses out

71

of the young, the most recent writers see the schools as in the clutch of similar devils, who similarly must be exorcised if the promise of education is to be fulfilled.

Who killed our Eden? We hear from the humanists, especially the young, that technology and the computer have done it, from the behaviorists that a mushy humanist approach has done it, from the secularists that religion and the churches have done it, from the churches that the exclusion of prayer and religious instruction has done it. We hear from the "basic education" groups that educational progressivism has done it, and from the progressives that a narrow literalism of teaching has done it. We hear from the discipline-minded that a runaway permissiveness has done it, and from the liberal school reformers that a mindless, repressive control by school boards and parents' groups has done it. We hear from the traditionalists that drugs, sex, and violence have done it, and from the counter-culture that a revived Puritanism has done it. We hear from the right wing that the bleeding-heart liberals and the Communists have done it, and from the class theorists of the left that the corporations, the dominant state elites and capitalist society have done it. We hear from the militant blacks that the white racists have done it, and from the militant whites that open admissions, black pressures, and the collapse of educational standards have done it. Finally we hear from free-wheeling school critics that bureaucracy and the joylessness of instruction have done it.

Of these artillery barrages there is one that has most vividly captured the imagination of the younger and more radical critics. It is the attack on the ruling classes as the manipulators of the educational system.

There has been a minor flurry of revival in the class analysis of the school system, largely from the impetus of the New Left of the 1960s. The Marxist viewpoint has thus far developed few insights in this area, largely because education has mostly been a concern of the parents for their children and has become increasingly a concern of the American civic conscience about minority groups.

The reality is more complex than the Marxist attack allows for. The reality is: 1) that the question of ethnicity has come to dominate educational policy far more than has class distinction. Some Marxist writers have tried to absorb the ethnic hostilities and clashes of interests into class hostilities and clashes of interests. But it won't wash. The two concepts intersect on the condition of the subclass of the black poor, but only there.

2) The class issue—to the extent that it exists in education—is not between the big corporations and the exploited poor, but between the lower-middle and upper-middle classes, white and black alike. The upper-middle segment of whites has done its best to fight for integration, which the lower-middle whites resist. The lower-middle and poverty level blacks often feel happier in their own neighborhood schools, but the upper-middle blacks see integration as a question of principle.

3) An intensive study of the watershed integration case, *Brown* v. *Board of Education,* such as Richard Kluger's *Simple Justice* (1976), shows the Supreme Court—which ought to be a bastion of the dominant class—scrupulously laying aside individual and doctrinal differences to present a unanimous front in overruling past precedents. Even the centrist and conservative Nixon-appointed judges, who have tried to reverse the Warren Court's rulings on criminal justice, have maintained its rulings on desegregation. Despite pockets of local resistance to Court-enforced desegregation, there is little likelihood of a major reversal of judicial direction.

4) One argument of the class theorists is that class domination is subtler in education than in its more naked forms, and that it takes the form of adjusting

the students to the status quo. Every society tries to educate for adjustment to the society by transmitting loyalty and value systems intact. But America does it not more but less than most. The life adjustment school of educational thinking has been very much on the defensive, and the attack on social conformity has been pervasive. On any deliberate level the American school system has done less than, let us say, the French or Germans, and certainly less than Communist or Third World countries, to flatten out and homogenize the minds of the young. Few school systems have tried as consciously and tenaciously to educate for individual identity and dissent, even for rebellion. The history of the 1960s, with its college revolts, its student activisms, and its counter-culture is pretty good evidence that the effort succeeded, with a Sorcerer's Apprentice overflow of success. The damage caused to the school system—higher and lower—was a self-inflicted wound.

More serious than the attacks from the intellectual left are those from the people as a whole. The 1975 Gallup survey of public attitudes toward education, as seen by a cross-section poll, shows the top ten problems to be these: 1) Lack of discipline; 2) Busing; 3) Money; 4) Hard to get good teachers; 5) School and class size; 6) Drugs; 7) Poor curriculum; 8) Crime/vandalism/stealing; 9) Lack of adequate facilities; and 10) Pupils' lack of interest.

What stands out immediately is the harsh mood this list shows toward what used to be called progressivism in education and has now been renamed "permissiveness" by its critics. Items 1, 2, 6, and 8—discipline, busing, drugs, crime and vandalism—belong in this category. I suspect that item 10 does also—the pupils' lack of interest and motivation ascribed to wrong-headed teaching. Almost certainly the vote on item 7—the poor curriculum—suggest the same dour view: that the curriculum isn't strong enough on the basics and includes too much liberal, useless, and even corrupting stuff.

This view is borne out by the response to another question, about sending children to a special— independent—public school with strict discipline, a strict dress code, and a curriculum emphasis on the three Rs. The overall vote was 57 percent in favor, 33 percent against. What is more notable was that there was a majority for it from every region. Every educational level, every community size, from whites and nonwhites, and from both sexes.

Just as revealing was the response on the decline in students' test scores. The four leading reasons given were: lack of motivation, 29 percent; lack of home and school discipline, 28 percent; inadequate emphasis on basics in the curriculum, 22 percent; inadequate teachers, 21 percent.

There you have the picture in the minds of young and older adults about the American school system. What it amounts to is that 200 years after independence a growing number of people feel that somewhere along the road America took the wrong turn on education, and that the result is low behavior standards in the schools, lagging interest, and poor testing results. In effect the people want the schools to turn back to where the roads forked, and take the one they feel we abandoned—the road toward strict discipline, hard work, basic no-nonsense subjects, traditional values.

Just as striking is the contrast between the view of the school system which class theorists like Ivan Illich, Herbert Marcuse, and Jonathan Kozol take, and the view that a cross-section of the people themselves take. It doesn't follow, of course, that either view is therefore right or wrong. But the gap is especially striking because it suggests how alienated the class theorists are from the actual discontents and felt needs of the people.

If in fact the school system has steadily gone downhill in recent decades no survey of attitudes can tell us why. It can spot the discontents but not how to answer them. While there are differences of opinion in the nation about who and what corrupted our Eden, it is not a question that a public opinion poll can answer. Nor can the answer come from the schools of psychology which I canvassed above. It can come only from hard and sustained study of the place of the schools, and of educational forces outside the schools, in the larger civilizational setting.

As a preliminary approach one might ask whether what happened to the schools was due to what happened outside the schools—the loosening of family ties, the general lowering of standards, the increase in crime, the polarizing of ethnic tensions, the uprooting of the young from family and community, the breaking of the connections which form a web of relations for the developing person, the clash and confusion of values.

It is in the area of value systems, more than any other single area, that we may come closest to an answer. This was touched on in the poll. To one of the survey questions, about "instruction in the schools that would deal in the morals and moral behavior," the response was 72 percent in favor, 15 percent against.

As phrased, it might raise the thorny constitutional question of religion in the schools. But there can be an approach that would bypass any formal religious instruction. The real problem is how to bring the discussion of values into education without moralizing, without indoctrination and propaganda. It won't be easy. But to stay away from the values problem doesn't mean that the values problem stays away from us. The young are already swimming in a confused sea of values, by the very fact of being exposed to family and peer group interactions, to books, to press and film and TV. They are constantly battered by storms of values of which they are unaware.

The task ahead is for teacher and student to become

aware of the values problem, to treat the daily experience of life—public and private—as raw material for case studies in the clash of values, to turn education into a values dialogue, and thus to help in the shaping and internalizing of values.

A Beast in View: The Aims of Education

"All, all of a piece throughout,/Thy Chase had a Beast in View," wrote John Dryden. During most of American history, education has had a beast in view: one has only to read Jonathan Messerle's account of how Horace Mann, in setting up his school system, aimed to shape the minds of the young into civic members of the society. Before him Jefferson, much occupied with establishing the University of Virginia, had been equally clear about a different aim—that of shaping "an aristocracy of virtue and talent."

These were the polar statements of educational aims in America. One was a kind of *civism*—more than civil religion, less than statism. The other was a kind of elitism, but a very special kind, envisaging not an aristocracy of blood and privilege but a democratic elite, with constantly new resources of character and ability brought into the circulation of the elite. The two were never very far apart. Jefferson was a democratic aristocrat, at once a tribune of the people and a polished cosmopolite. Horace Mann, moved by the currents of the new nationalism, cared not only about the social cohesion that the school system could achieve out of the children of the diverse ethnic, religious, and class groups, but also about their individual pursuit of happiness.

There have been other statements of what the aims of education should be. One is the Platonic view—that it should be a tool of the (city-) state. It was also the Prussian ideal, as it has been in every military society. It went far in Plato's statement of the role of the Guardians.

This view found, despite Plato's anguish at the death of Socrates, a wholly logical outcome in that death, for if the shaping of the minds of the young is toward the glory and strength of the state, and if a teacher corrupts them (as Socrates was charged with), then he has indeed betrayed the state. Socrates saw and embraced this logic and met his death stoically in order not to falsify it. Despite John Stuart Mill's *On Liberty* he didn't die for freedom but for subversion. The two were linked, however, in the sense that, if you accept education as a tool of the state, then every form of teaching that asserts or encourages cognitive freedom is a subversive art.

In America it doesn't have to be, because—broadly speaking—education has not cast itself in the role of a tool of the state, nor has the state asserted its right to use such a tool. True, an absolute libertarian might assert that the very fact of compulsory schooling already makes it a state tool. But this confuses state power as an enforcing agency for school attendance, with state power as the aim of education.

There are two related problems about education: one is its aims, and the other is how best to organize its governance in order to achieve those aims. Focusing on the former, one must stress, at least in theory, the difference for education between a consensus state, where government is by the people and they never relinquish control of it, and a class-party state where the decisions are made by a party bureaucracy and the only control is the ultimate one of the threat of revolution. If there were an ideal state and society, the interests of both would also be the interests of students, teachers, and parents. There would then be a heavenly harmony between aims and governance in education, and all would be well. But in the earthly state and society there are discords, not harmony, and the voices raised about education are dissonances. Hence the need for being clear about aims and organization.

Americans have on the whole tended to resolve the problem by muting the role of the state—even a consensual state—in their formulation of educational aims, and in practice by applying the principle of reverse hierarchy. Which means that the lesser evil, for the governance of education, lies in vesting it in the lower governmental forms (local) rather than the higher ones (state, federal). Since the states have at times insisted on a role in curriculum decision (courses on the nature of Communism and democracy), and the federal government sets standards for "affirmative action" on personnel policies, the American distrust of state interests as educational goals has been confirmed.

There remains what I should call the Periclean question. If Pericles was right in saying that politics is character, and that education is character formation, then it follows that the essence of education is political. That is a better way of putting the problem than the traditional one of saying that education must be a state instrument. Yet even in the subtler form there is a fatal flaw in the syllogism above. Let us agree that politics is character, but who is to decide what kind of character structure in the young is best for the polity, whether it be the heavenly or the earthly city?

There are three approaches to this question of education for civic character formation, and they flow into one another. One is what Charles E. Merriam and the cluster of scholars around him at the University of Chicago in the 1920s and early 1930s used to call "the making of citizens." They did a number of notable studies on the ways in which citizens have been trained, both in democracies and dictatorships. Yet they left no abiding impact, either on political or educational theory, largely because the later experience with nuclear secrecy and the McCarthyite disloyalty hunt frightened many thinkers away from this strain of thought. Granted that loyalty—to family, friends, community, nation—is a value deeply embedded in the traditional value system, Americans concluded that there are better ways of shaping it than by educating deliberately for national loyalty.

A second approach is the effort to educate for social cohesiveness and not exclusively for individual grati- fication and fulfillment. A strong case can be made for such an aim. It follows from the modern versions of the "social contract" theories of law and the state: that in order to get their protection from the state of nature, whose vileness and brutality Hobbes de- scribed in his classic passage in *Leviathan,* we give up enough of our freedoms to make law possible. Since laws in themselves have not proved capable of maintaining a social order, it follows that they will be enforceable only if a climate of social cohesiveness (sometimes called "civility") can be achieved. In such a climate—to be fostered by educating for it as the prime aim—what Robert Nisbet calls the "social bond" is strengthened, and the old social contract takes on new meaning.

A third approach has to do with the viability of the society itself. It is closely related to the cohesive- ness aim, but takes on a sharper focus at a time of troubles like the present, when America is passing through a succession of crises, some of which may loom as of a life-and-death nature. During the 1940s and early 1950s, Americans were in a quest for their identity in a postwar world and were inquiring about their national purpose. Someone put the question to Dean Acheson. His answer was classic: "Our purpose, sir, is to survive—and perchance to flourish."

He was logically right to put survival first, since there can be no flourishing unless a society survives to flourish in. His answer to the question of the aim of education was thus one of shaping the national character so that the nation can survive, hence flourish. Yet by a deeper logic—or a deeper psycho-logic—it isn't a one-way sequence. Unless there are good life chances for flourishing there will be few incentives for national survival, especially for those—the young,

poor, disadvantaged—in whose psyches a belief system has to be established and strengthened.

This may seem close to a mystique of the mass
of people, yet I don't intend it as such, but only as
a way of putting the reality principle that every society
must be a belief system in order to survive and flourish.
Education has a role in shaping that belief system,
but the question of fairness and equal access in the
functioning of the society also has a role.

There are statements of educational aims which do
rest on a mystique of the mass. When they are not
Whitmanesque, with a leaves-of-grass mysticism, they
are heavily soaked in the pathos of human wret-
chedness among the subclass of the children of the
deprived. This often has a purgative effect, in relieving
a sense of guilt, but it does little for educational
thinking. This is true also of a related theory, that
education should be a tool of the class struggle, and
that its effectiveness must be judged by whether it
helps bring about a hard-core revolution. One can
understand how some class theorists would subordi-
nate their concern for education to their concern for
dissolving a consensus democracy to replace it with
a proletarian dictatorship, but it is hard to see why
they should expect the rest of the educational community to acquiesce in such a dissolution.

Something of the same applies to the idea that all
schools are instruments of class and state, and that
society is best deschooled. The trouble with this vision
is that when a school vacuum is achieved, what is
likely to move into the vacuum is the fiercest kind
of ethnic, religious, and particularist intensity, in a
rivalry to use state funds to achieve the ends of the
particular group. The result would be not greater but
less social cohesiveness, and a further crumbling of
the cement of a society which has already crumbled
enough.

One could, of course, sweep all these cobwebby
purposes away and reach for simplicities. A suit was

brought recently by a student against Columbia University, on the ground that it had contracted to give him wisdom and had not delivered on the contract. One can sympathize with his sense of frustration, but alas, there are no bales of wisdom, wired and crated, for us to feed on in the pastures of an educational heaven. There are only the resources of creativeness in life and thought that enable us to ponder on the nature of wisdom and how it can best be—not achieved, but approached.

There is another statement of educational aim which is breathtaking in its simplicity. It is Friedrich Nietzsche's—that the aim of education is to discover and nourish geniuses. Like most theories it tells as much about the thinker's self-image as about anything else. Yet Nietzsche's formulation, extreme as it is, has some point as a counter-idea in a society where mediocrity reigns in the school system. I shall return to his insights on education in a later passage on the carriers of promise and a democratic elite. Here, I wish only to suggest its place in the larger cluster of aims.

My own view, implicit throughout this book, is that the aim of education should be to teach and learn how to aim at an education, for the whole person, in the total life span. To put it more fully, it is to bring all the resources of the cognitive, intuitive, and creative life of the society and the self to bear on shaping the mind, psyche, and person of every member of the society, so as to develop both the self and the society. Education must aim at persons who are fulfilling and fulfilled, in a society which they thereby nourish and strengthen. Unless education is thus a fertilizing ground for the whole life cycle in the whole civilization, it will not have explored its true aim.

Power and Values: The Government of Education

For a time, in America, there was an awkwardness about recognizing that education—far from being nonpolitical—is steeped in politics. Every year, every day, the battle is over who will wield the power in this far-flung fragmented network of little principalities that we call school districts and school systems. Will it be the local superintendents, the school boards, the mayors, the state commissioners, the federal bureaus, the school administrators, the teachers, the parents, the pressure groups, the unions, the unofficial local power elites?

Which of them runs the schools? The answer is, of course, that all of them do to some extent, none of them wholly or exclusively. There is a fragmented pluralism of power distribution. Broadly teachers and administrators run the school system, within a frame set by superintendents and school boards who are to some extent guided by the informal local elites, within a still looser frame set by political leaders and by state and federal officials, with parents, pressure groups, and unions able to say No by their veto power, even though their claims and desires are not met from day to day.

This is a very American picture in the intricacy of its patterning. But questions still remain: why the power struggles are waged over particular issues, why they are so intense and sustained, why they whip up a fury of emotions?

Economic motives play a role, since school costs form the largest single item in local and state budgets. One may speak of the political economy of education in America, since economic issues—especially of school financing—are fought out in political terms. On the principle that those who pay the piper decide the tune, local financing and local control of education have been interlocked.

This has had two major consequences. It has meant sharp differentials in the per capita expenditures on education from school district to school district, depending on the wealth or poverty of the community and the slimness or strength of its tax base. Recent

court decisions have brought this into question because
of the unequal impact on the education that children
get. The system has also meant that on school issues
the voters may be voting their tax pocketbooks instead
of the welfare of the young, especially if they have
no children of their own currently in the public
schools.

But the important reason for the intensity of school
politics lies outside the economic motive. It must be
seen in a values context. Education is America's most
important industry because its product is the future
lives of the young. If Americans feel satisfied with
the product they will gladly pay for it. If they don't
the sense of being cheated can rise to a fury. Hence
the cry for "accountability," which—despite the way
many teachers feel—need not be for a crass cost
accounting but for a total one. "We have given you
our children. What have you done with them?"

This is one area where the *value* terms may be used
in their double sense: value received for value given.
Or—using a play on words—if the parents have made
an (economic) *value* input, they feel entitled to a (life)
values output.

It is this concern for the children that makes educational politics to so high a degree symbolic politics.
For every victory and defeat, on whichever side of
the conflict it may come, seems multiplied in importance because of its probable—perhaps even irreversi-
ble—impact on children's lives. As with all political
wars, the stakes of the struggle are power—in this
case power over educational decision making. But
what gives the struggle its intensity is that these
decisions bear so strongly on two sets of outcomes
for the students—on their learning habits and skills,
their jobs and careers, their income level and life
placement, but also on their characters and their life
values. Both of these clusters of outcomes might in
a sense be called the stakes-within-the-stakes.

To see the struggle as basically one between teachers

and parents, or professionals and nonprofessionals—
as many on both sides tend to do—is to view it too
narrowly and in a largely outmoded frame. The more
intense struggles are between parents and parents, with
the professionals drawn into them, often unwarily and
unwillingly. Sometimes also the struggles are intra-
professional—between teachers and administrators, or
even teachers and teachers, and this time the non-
professional "outsiders" may be drawn into the vortex,
often unwarily and unwillingly. Put these together
and you get a bewildering number of possible per-
mutations of struggle.

Aside from problems of integration, busing, testing,
and "affirmative action," which I shall discuss in the
next section, there are basically two battle line-ups
in the educational struggles. In recent studies they
have been called the "bimodal" and "trimodal." In
the broadest terms the power struggle has been between the lower-middle and upper-middle classes,
with the white-black divisions cutting across both.
Sometimes however it is useful to see it as trimodal:
blue collar, white collar (middle-middle), and upper-
middle.

In the Levittown (pre-fab planned suburbs) battles
the tendency was for blue collar and white collar to
unite against upper-middle, in a struggle of traditional
values and "basics" as against progressivism. In the
more affluent suburbs, often heavily Jewish, the progressives have largely won, often carrying liberal
administrators with them. In the suburbs opened up
for black migrations from the cities in the sixties, the
dominant alliance has been between white and black
progressives, but in the harsher economic climate of
the early 1970s the blue-collar elements of both races
began to assert their strength and their traditional
values perspective.

In the big cities the questions of control of teaching
were often overshadowed by the ethnic issues. Usually
the alignment of struggle was between the blacks and

their upper-middle white allies on one side and the white ethnics on the other. This was clearest in a city like Boston or Detroit. But in Chicago the skill of the city officials in recruiting loyalties across ethnic lines kept the polarizing from getting sharp. In New York the dominant issue for a time was that of decentralized school district administration as against the clinging of the professionals and unions (largely Jewish) to the centralized controls.

To depict the power struggles largely in class and ethnic terms, as I have too briefly done, misses some of the subtler values aspects. For example, in suburb and big city alike there was often an opposition between the sectors of the community where the family system was largely stable and those where it was unstable, with a high jobless rate and single-parent (usually mother) homes. In the stable situation the stress was on traditional values, in the other the value system was highly vulnerable if not wholly crumbled.

There has been a micro-politics in the American school system, as well as a macro-politics—a politics of the classroom community as well as of the larger community. In fact one could argue that the only meaningful struggles are those that take place inside the schoolhouse and classroom, that the others are only reflected images, like the shadows in Plato's cave.

Take as an instance what one might call the ecology of the classroom. Questions of open space and of the open classroom (the two need not be identical) as against the more traditional graded and specialized classrooms represent a clash between holistic and segmented approaches to the student. This is substantially true also of team as against individual teaching. It cuts even more deeply on the question of cross-age-group organization of the classroom, as one phase of the theory that heterogeneous groupings make possible a better learning and growing experience than homogeneous ones. They set parameters, as it were, for both peer group and ethnic group influence.

I feel strongly that the government of the nation begins in the local community, and the government of the local community in its classrooms. One could apply something like a Levi-Strauss structural approach to it.

It is here, within the intellectual-social-values structuring of the classroom, that the self-concept of student and teacher alike is shaped, and here that the concept of *the other* is also shaped. It is here that both the authority concept and the anarchy concept emerge, the sense of limits to human behavior and the sense of freedom. It is here that student and teacher alike learn about taking risks and playing it safe, about adventuring and routinizing, about fellow feeling and self-centeredness, about living *with* technology or living *by* it, about reaching a consensus or seeking to impose one's will, about working with the going institutions while seeking to improve them, or being estranged from them, about coping with the pathetic and the tragic in life or crumbling before them.

Put in these terms, the opposition between the "traditional" and "progressive" positions in the power struggles and value struggles of the community seems much too simplistic. The government of education does in fact get entangled with the question of value shaping. But to see it in good-guy/bad-guy terms is to see not the reality but a caricature.

Access, Rigidity, and Human Worth

At this point I must risk a bit of autobiography. I recall an evening I had, some years ago on a visit to Warsaw, with a number of writers, artists, teachers. The chairman of the evening referred politely to my *America as a Civilization,* which had been published several years earlier. "We haven't had a chance to get your book translated," he said. "But could you tell us in a single word what is the essence of American civilization?" I thought hard and fast, reviewing all the possible concepts in the American tradition—

freedom, democracy, equality, tolerance, consensus, justice, dynamism, enterprise.

Then I heard myself say, "Access." The chairman laughed: "We have heard of American *success* but not of *access*." I explained: "You see, we have a Declaration of Independence which says that all men are born free and equal. I hope they are born free everywhere and will remain free. But they are born not equal but unequal, with unequal abilities and potentials. This doesn't apply to categories, like race, religion, income, sex, but only to individual differences. Every teacher, parent, employer knows it. But we also have the idea in America that we must all have *equal access to equal life chances,* so that every one of these unequally born youngsters gets a chance to develop his unequal potentials to the full."

Of the two meanings of equality I didn't mean equality of result, which no society can underwrite for its members; I mean equality of opportunity, which a caring society can in fact provide. Democracy does not mean equal abilities or equal wealth or income or life expressiveness. It should mean only that young Americans should not have to grapple hopelessly with the man-made pathos of life, but have an equal chance to enjoy the fulfilling and face the tragic in life.

One could rewrite the history of America in the past two hundred years as a succession of efforts to come ever closer to a society of equal access, from the Jeffersonian and Jacksonian Revolutions through the Civil War, the Populist movement of the 1880s and 1890s, the intellectual renaissance of the turn of the century, the New Nationalism of Theodore Roosevelt, the New Freedom of Wilson, the New Deal and the Fair Deal of Franklin Roosevelt and Harry Truman, the New Frontier and the Great Society of John Kennedy and Lyndon Johnson. I have used the political slogans, both for brevity and to express the fact that political-social reform movements get what strength they possess from their congruence with both the discontents and the passionate strivings of the people themselves.

Somewhere in the mid-1960s, at the height of the wave of antiwar and civil rights activisms that marked the decade, the tradition of equal access achieved its high point of legislative success in the passage of the Civil Rights Act of 1964 and the Voting Rights Act of 1965. The acts transformed the access situation in three areas—schooling opportunity, job opportunity, and residential opportunity. Clearly all three are related: residence patterns bring certain schools within (or outside) the reach of particular families, job patterns make certain school or residence opportunities viable (or not), school patterns form the underpinning of job or educational achievement. Add to these three a fourth—voting equality—which gave a new voting consciousness and power to minority groups, and which made the other three more possible.

This might have ushered in a healthy new period of educational advance as part of a multifront social advance. But it was not to be. Instead of limiting the new programs to whatever was necessary to make access to equal opportunity equal, there was a runaway effect which often happens in the history of social movements. The zeal, without which the movements for change could not have succeeded, carries over after the runner has reached his goal. To change the image, the organism—in its effort to counteract an unhealthy condition—overdoes the effect, creates unhealth in the opposite direction, and still has to find its way to an equilibrium.

What happened was that the idea of affirmative action, sound in itself, got into the hands of civil rights partisans, federal administrators (especially in Health, Education, and Welfare), school and university administrators, and public opinion makers, who spelled it out to mean something never intended and at variance with the whole American tradition. They took it to mean a guarantee of statistical equality of result, especially in admission quotas, and in employment quotas. The base used for statistical parities was the proportion of various ethnic, racial, and sexual groups to the total population of whatever area—local or national—was held relevant. To achieve this the recruiting of public school teachers and of university faculties and staff had to focus—under threat of federal cancellation of contracts and subsidies—on the race and sex of the applicants rather than on their record and indicated ability.

However generous the motives behind this development, it has been mischievous in its effect, at least for education. Instead of fulfilling access theory it violates access theory, since it shuts off equal access for students, teachers, and administrators who are not members of the favored groups. It introduces a measure of decision in admission, recruiting, and employment policies—that of statistical parity—which undercuts the basic traditions of rewarding effort and ability. It replaces the past antiminority discrimination with an equally unjust affirmative or reverse discrimination. It abandons the idea of treating human beings in terms of their human selves and treats them instead as items of ascribed categories, thereby making them objects, not subjects. It revives memories of past quota systems, especially for Jews whose immigrant forebears had to suffer from job and educational quotas in Europe, and for many others who were exiles from various totalitarian regimes for reasons of religious and political conscience.

In the American case the history of fighting educational bias has been one of healthy intent. Notably the attack against the whole broad front of discrimination was spearheaded by the attack on school segregation, and the victory won in the great desegregation case—*Brown* v. *Board of Education*—was a victory also against bias in every other area. The whole liberal community, white and black, intellectual, legal, and political, participated in shaping the strategy that led to victory in the case (see Richard Kluger's intensive intellectual history of the case, *Simple Justice*). The decision itself was a triumph of the American conscience, American social flexibility, and the judicial statesmanship of Chief Justice Warren and Justices Frankfurter and Black, who agreed that on so monumental a case a decision by a divided Court would be fatal.

From the perspective of this book there are three comments worth adding. One is that the men and women who worked at the whole movement of thought and action resulting in the *Brown* decision must somehow have scrounged up a good education, to have been able to carry it off. A second is that it was a triumph of healthy values over somewhat squeaky constitutional law, as Alexander Bickel has shown in *The Supreme Court and the Idea of Progress*. The third is that, along with whole movement for a more equal access to life chances, it showed a remarkable adaptability in the American educational and social organism.

The danger is, however, that the whole direction since the early 1970s has endangered the health of the organism by making it too rigid. In the history of organisms, whether biological, intellectual, or social, rigidity spells death. In the effort to break up the rigidity of antiminority bias in education, we are coming close to establishing another rigidity—that of statistical parity between school and job results and the size of the constituent elements in the population. This becomes a new form of segregation, using the same basic logic of categories rather than of individual human worth which the original segregation used. The task ahead is once more to desegregate and derigidify the social organism.

The difficulties are great but surmountable. Somehow the American intellectual community got itself bogged down on the question of whether the differential IQs between white and black test subjects are due to genetic or cultural determinisms. The question of which set of factors is more strongly determining is one that has been around a long time, on issues of talent, genius, life achievement, disease, and various personality sets. In the climate of ethnic struggle the overassertive work of Jensen, Shockley, and Herrnstein took on threatening overtones as perceived by some sensitive black scholars and their liberal white allies.

The best way to put the current state of knowledge about race and intelligence would run somewhat as follows: that there are genetic differences, in the whole spectrum of mankind, in terms of the response of the brain (both cognitive and intuitive) to various environments and stimuli; that over long stretches of time, environments have an impact on the potentials of the brain, but that by the same token planned changes in the environment—over short as well as long time spans—can bring about changes in brain response; that there are no given racial genetic limits to brain potential which operate under every set of circumstances; that no statement about the intelligence of groups can be made which doesn't reckon with this factor of plasticity.

In the areas of literature, the arts, entertainment, sports, the media, political leadership, religion, and the whole world of the imagination the blacks have held their own in the competitive struggle, and sometimes better than their own. They are starting to do so in the social sciences, like history, economics, politics, and psychology, in the medical and legal professions, in business. If they have not yet made their mark in philosophy and in the physical and mathematical sciences, we still have no way of knowing whether the determining factors are cultural and environmental or genetic. In any event the outcome should have no effect on educational policy, which should be directed toward human worth, not categories.

Another intellectual mare's nest has been the debate over whether education does or does not level out social and economic inequalities in their impact on a life career. Christopher Jencks performed a service with his book, *Inequality*, by challenging the American myth that if you go to school you will somehow get ahead. By a tough-minded round-up of studies he discovered what equally tough-minded critics might have suspected—that others, from more advantaged backgrounds, will also get ahead and will get ahead faster because of friendship, contacts, influence, and other intangibles of social situation and interaction.

Jencks had his own angle of vision in the book—his belief that only a fundamental restructuring of the society can achieve changes which the educational process in itself cannot achieve. But from the angle of vision of youngsters from families with low educational levels it still remains true that a better education than their parents got is a must for them. It may or may not enable them to advance much: that depends on personal factors. But without education—given the knowledge revolution and the technological revolutions of our time—their lot would be considerably worse.

I might add, from my own angle of vision—and from the earlier discussion of the aims of education— that the real question is not whether an education enables you to catch up economically and socially with others, but whether it helps you to be more interesting to yourself and others, to develop your own inner resources, and to lead a more expressive life. To answer those questions we would need a very different array of studies and figures from those that Jencks marshalled.

In the realm of social myth the belief that education is worthwhile, whether for making a living or making a life, is not likely to be easily shaken. It is a life necessity in America because the whole society is an educational society, and because the common experi-

ence of ordinary people bears it out constantly, whatever the learned surveys. This is true also for a
latter-day America which will have to wrestle with
the ethnicity concept in a multi-ethnic society. We
have moved far from the "melting pot" paradigm, and
have come to accept the concept of retaining ethnic
identity even while accepting the larger integrated
culture. In Michael Novak's term, the white as well
as the black ethnics are proving "unmeltable."

Any educational thinker worth his salt, in the re-
mainder of this century, will have to study this whole
class and ethnic landscape with a cool eye. He will
be sympathetic to human needs and worth whether
among the white or black ethnics or even the now
neglected ones—those of stock from the earliest im-
migrations—but he will be critical of the advocacy
thinkers who start with an unexamined bias and move
toward inevitable but unproved conclusions. Advocacy law and advocacy public relations, like advocacy
politics, are understandable. But advocacy social and
educational theory is a contradiction in terms and
self-defeating.

The difficulty about advocacy is its rigidity. It was
true of both sides of the busing controversy in the
mid-1970s and interfered with a possible solution.
In time we may arrive at one, but only if we take
an organismic approach and understand that the
school, the neighborhood, and the ethnic groups involved are all social organisms.

The segregated school was too constricted as an
organism, too limited in the experience it offered
students and teachers, too damaging to their self-image
and their sense of worth. Some of the integrated schools
are on the way to becoming healthy organisms, but
not others. The trouble with busing was that it was
too artificial a way to create a new school organism,
which is not surprising, given the American belief
that technologies can solve social problems. Its rigidity
as an instrument was all the stronger because it came

in through the judges rather than the legislatures (the latter had passed up their chance to desegregate the schools) and their intervention took on the character of constitutional law rather than the more flexible one of legislative enactment.

Desegregation helped the black community as an organism by giving it a sense that it could win some social battles, and it was accepted by most of the white communities. But busing as instrument proved clumsy and damaging to both, and awakened a responsive militancy among the white ethnic communities, damaging the neighborhood as organism.

The path back to organismic wholeness will be long and hard. But it will be possible if all the groups keep two concepts in mind—the organism and human worth, rather than category thinking. Once these are firmly grasped there are no inherent reasons why the educational and social energies of the groups that make up "the new ethnicity" should be in conflict. Good will, fellow feeling, civility, and a sense of common purpose can be summoned on both sides. There is a principle of homeostasis that works in developed organisms, sometimes even in the social organism. But if some collective human will and intelligence are mustered to help the process the outcome will be clearer.

4

Toward a Values Theory

The Values Ethos: Traditional and Challenger Systems

I t is time to pull together and make explicit what is implicit in everything I have written here about value formation and its relation to teaching, learning, and living together. Man is neither a fallen archangel nor a risen ape, although his endowment contains much of each. In every phase of his being, for good or ill, he is a value-receiving, value-choosing, value-carrying, value-shaping, value-transmitting, value-binding animal.

I use the *values* concept in a number of related senses: the questions that we put to life, the assessments (valuations) of worth that we make to guide us in life choices and decisions, the structurings of worth and unworth that we seek to impose on the flux of experience and our relations with others, the ways in which we seek meanings in our lives, reaching out to tie events and transactions in meaningful relationships.

In every era, in every culture and civilization, these meanings and questions—and to some extent answers to the questions—have been woven into *value clusters,* and the clusters in turn into *value systems.* Thus one may speak of a cluster around the worth of *work,* or of *achievement,* or of *acquisitiveness,* or of *pleasure* or *happiness,* or of *security,* or of the *military virtues,* or of *service to God,* or of *fellow feeling* and helpfulness to others and to humanity. Each of these clusters, or systems, takes on the character of the socially sanctioned *oughts* of the society, and becomes an ethos. Thus we may have a work ethos, an achievement ethos, a pecuniary ethos, a hedonic ethos, a security ethos, a military ethos, a Godliness ethos, a socialist or altruist ethos.

All of these are clearly related to deep drives and needs within human beings. They related variously to the need to assert selfhood, to achieve and be effective, to cope and wrestle with self and others, to be secure, to belong, to worship, to believe. In a primarily religious age, or a primarily economic or political one, or a primarily hedonic one, the prevailing value system will at once shape and reflect the ethos of the age. It may well be that they form the most significant feature of a civilization, giving a people its national character, in the sense of what it most cares about and most lives by, and therefore its distinguishing long-range traits, beyond the quirky or ephemeral.

As the common heritage of a people, forming the atmosphere within which they live and have their being, the value structure—binding time, tradition, strivings, and relationships in the present, hopes for the future—gives a society a large measure of the cohesiveness it possesses. When the value structure erodes over time, under the battering of the tests and skepticisms to which it is exposed, the cohesions erode. When the value structure is broken, by swift revolutionary change whether from within or without, the cohesion is broken. In fact, the deepest element of a process of revolutionary change-from-within, such as America experienced from the late 1950s well into the 1970s, lies in the siege undergone by the traditional ethos, under attack from the cohorts of the skeptics, the alienated, the true believers in some challenger ethos, and the nihilists—the disbelievers in any ethos.

The remarkable thing about the American belief

system is not that it is starting to crumble under these attacks, but that it has held on as long and tenaciously as it has. Whether we call it the Puritan ethos, or the Protestant ethos, or the Judeao-Christian ethos, or even the capitalist-democratic ethos, the crucial fact about it is that it came out of a complex of three closely interwoven strands of life activity—the religious, the economic, and the sexual. It goes back in America to Benjamin Franklin and Cotton Mather, in Europe to John Calvin, John Bunyan, and Martin Luther, to the capitalist merchants and entrepreneurs of the Continent, and the British and American tool makers, inventors, and captains of industry.

Thus the carriers of the traditional ethos in America were interlaced class and religious movements. Its sense of vocation, work, inner discipline, and commitment came out of the Calvinist-Puritan revolutions in Europe since the sixteenth and seventeenth centuries and has been periodically renewed by new religious "awakenings." Its economic roots came further out of the early capitalisms of Europe, as described in their linkages with religion by Sombart, Weber, and Tawney, and as renewed notably in the early and high capitalism of America. Its liberal-democratic-individualist character came out of the middle-class revolutions of the seventeenth and eighteenth centuries in Europe and their spokesmen among the moral philosophers in England and France, and out of the planter-tradesman-lawyer revolution of 1776 in America, and it was renewed by the Jeffersonian-Jacksonian revolutions of the early nineteenth century. Its sexual mores were closely linked with its religious teachings and economic virtues, from the images of godliness, vocation, postponement of gratification, heaven and hell, the centrality of the family, and the primacy of male roles in religious and economic life.

The ethos of any society is built thus into its history, its daily life and power relationships, and its religion, myths, and imaginings. It is not surprising that at any

given time it seems to embody the eternal verities
and evoke an almost unquestioning belief in its validity. Obviously the beliefs slacken and change, and the
eternal verities prove temporary, to be displaced by
others that seem equally unchallengeable and eternal—until they in turn are displaced.

Yet it would be wrong to conclude that there is
a complete relativism about value systems, that—as
the Emperor Augustine believed about religions—any
value system will do, provided it holds belief. There
is always the question of the relation of the value
system to the society and the people in it, at that
stage in their history. Like the falcon they must—after
their widening gyres—return to the falconer. To
change the figure, if they move too far from the soil
of the human community in which they are rooted,
too far from the needs of the society and of man's
human endowment, they are bound to be challenged
and in time displaced.

There are times when the congruity between a value
system and the social and human needs of the society
is at its best, in the sense that the values and needs
do the least damage to each other and are nourishing
one to the others. At that point, which happens rarely
in the history of a civilization and a value system,
we may speak of an optimal values situation. There
may even be a succession of such periods, each with
its special kind of congruity—in the American instance
perhaps during the Era of Good Feelings in the 1820s
and 1830s, and again at the turn of the century, and
still again in the 1940s and 1950s of the Truman-Ei-
senhower years. If there is great adaptability both in
the society and the value system in the decades ahead
there may be another such period, but the greater
likelihood is for a diminishing congruity between
values and needs, and a steady process of erosion
of the old and encroachment of the new.

There has been no Oswald Spengler to trace the
rise and fall of value systems as he did of civilizations,

nor have American historians dealt with the history of American value systems. A history there has been, with a story of conflict that lacks the clangor of military conflict yet had a fatefulness in it which reached deeper and ramified farther than the outcome of wars.

The people who came from the unsettling of Europe to settle America found a value system already established—that of the indigenous Indian tribes. They brought with them their own systems, which were variants of the larger European ethos. They brought—and developed—a Puritan ethos in New England, a Quaker one in Pennsylvania, a Catholic one in Maryland, a Cavalier one in Virginia and the Carolinas. There were common elements between them, but also critical differences. The men and women who were transported from Africa in the holds of slave ships brought a still different cluster of values variants from their tribal homes. Those who came in later centuries and decades from the Mediterranean and East European societies, from the twelve corners of the earth, brought still different values traditions to add to the amalgam. The history of America has been the history, writ large, of the educational efforts, in school and home and wherever else, to transmit varying combinations of this richly competing, conflicting, and contradictory values material.

A central pattern did emerge, and it got itself called the traditional system because it got most deeply and strongly rooted and because it lasted. More than any other pattern it was the one transmitted, taught, internalized. But it would be wrong to see its boundaries as too sharply defined, just as it would be wrong to think of it as emerging full grown, like Minerva from the head of Zeus.

It was a historical product, with all the ragged edges and loose ends that characterize living entities in history. The values of the Indians were largely neglected: they were a road not taken. Yet recently, with the counter-culture of the young, and with a new sense

of worth in the pacific, nonmaterialist Indian values
and in the spirit world, there has been a degree of
return even to that road. The values of the blacks
influenced the southern culture over the generations,
because of the white system of child nurture, but it
did not reach into the larger culture until the strong
movements for ethnic equality during the New Deal
and after. The values of Jews and Catholics—each
of them part of a historical community that extended
beyond America and predated its settlement—were
basically at home with the Protestant ethic, but they
too became more penetrative of the larger culture in
latter-day America.

By the time of the late 1950s and 1960s there was
no longer an unchallenged values system. But those
decades made the challenge more decisive than it had
ever been. It came with the antiwar and antidraft
activisms, with the civil rights movement, but especially with an adversary movement against the prevailing culture so marked that Theodore Roszak's term
for it—the counter-culture—came to be accepted. If
I prefer the term *challenger values system,* it is to
move away from the showdown psychology among
the young at the time of generational struggle, and
also to make it more integrally part of the continuing
process of challenge which characterized the whole
history of American values.

The carriers of the challenger ethos were mainly
found in the intellectual class, and within that class
mainly among the elites of university students and
faculty. To some extent they were also found among
the elites of the black revolt. Together they gave the
new ethos a characteristic tone and content, with a
powerful appeal—by a contagion effect—to the ado-
lescents of high school age. It became clear that in
a period of values flux, what older siblings say and
do can be more powerful in the identification process
than what parents say, what teachers teach, what
preachers preach. Its impact was further heightened

by the multiplier effect of the media, carrying and spreading the generational message.

Revolutions in Values

With every critical change in a civilization, its value system changes as well. This has been true of the American civilization as of others. With changes in the history of technology, the economy, the ecological system, the family, and the churches, there have been corresponding changes in codes, morals, and beliefs. Thus the history of these institutional changes is a prerequisite for the history of values change. When changes in the triad above—codes, morals, and beliefs—are intense and pervasive and take place on a broad front, one may speak not only of values changes but of a values revolution.

We tend to think of it as a generational matter—a view which was strengthened in the 1960s by the perception of a dramatic generational gap. But this only pushes the question a step further, since it doesn't explain how or when such a gap arises. Nor does it explain why the generational change seems so erratic, with some younger generations more radical than their parents and some more conservative, some more sexually and emotionally expressive and some more constricted.

The key must be sought centrally in the nature of a new generation's experience, as compared with the earlier one. When the experience changes drastically—with wars, with changes in technology and the media, with changes in the family and in sexual knowledge and attitudes—the new generation uses that experience as a yardstick, to test how relevant and valid are the values being transmitted to it.

The flow of experience in which they are immersed, and their interchange of the meaning of that experience within their peer group, have raised certain questions in their minds about the society and about life in general and about themselves. It is the function of the value-shaping and value-transmitting agencies to give some tolerably satisfying answers to those questions. But if they don't—if parents, teachers, preachers, political leaders, media leaders fall short of explaining and giving meaning to the new experience—the new generation cuts its communication and values ties with the older. It is on its own.

At that point a generational values gap opens up. If it is wide enough, and if the generational differences are sharp and serious enough, a values crisis emerges. If the newer generation—and its allies among the older one—develops sharply new questions to put to life, and new answers to live by, then a values revolution is in process.

The process of values change has gone on continuously through the history of the colonies and the republic; the values revolutions have been relatively few. They have come when the new exposures and experience of the young have outrun the efforts of the values-keepers and values-transmitters to explain them, which means that they have come in periods of high acceleration in social change. But they have also required the means for making new explanations of their own, which means that they have come when changes in the intellectual climate and the media technology furnish them with those means. When these three elements converge—radically new social experience, generational distance, and new ways of formulating both questions and answers—then and only then do you get a values revolution.

I have suggested above that such a revolution took place in our time, starting in the late 1950s and stretching to the end of the 1960s. The generational conflict had broadly two aspects—the activist movements, which sought social change through passionate social action, and the movements of cultural revolution which sought change within the consciousness and life-style of individuals and trusted those inner changes to bring social change in their wake. The activists sought to overthrow the System and the Establishment and hoped for the coming of the Revolution. The cultural revolutionaries welcomed the greening which they sensed in America, and while many of them went along with a radical analysis of economic and political structures, they gave primacy to values change from within.

Of the two aspects, the first made more noise at the time, and won a number of victories in the radicalizing of attitudes, but it was the second—the cultural revolution—that left a longer range deposit of influence on the seventies and the decades to come, in the form of a values revolution.

The melancholy fact is that while the schools were the arena of these enactments in the form of angry classrooms, the turbulent schoolyard and school corridors, the campus riots and confrontations and the seizure of campus buildings, the scorn of dress codes, the new profiles of the young, their new vocabulary, the new pornography, the new sexual mores, the pregnancies, the drug mystique—they were unable to cope with them and largely unable to influence them. This is a measure at once of the failure of the educational system and of the task it must henceforth set for itself, both in the area of values direction.

To understand this we must understand that each of us lives in two universes. We all live in much the same outer universe, where the things that happen affect all of us, although in different ways, varying with the circumstances of our lives. But each also lives in an inner universe, of his longings, dreams, fears, aspirations, hang-ups, beliefs, commitments. This inner universe we share to some extent with others in our class or region, and especially our ethnic or age group. But in addition each of us has another inner universe which is the window through which we look out at the outer universe, and which defines the deepest aspects of our consciousness and personality.

The heart of this inner universe is inwardness, privacy, a fumbling toward value formation. It is the area of the largely unexamined, between the conscious and the unconscious. Since education aims at the examined life, it should find its most fertile material in the unexamined inner universe of the young. The teacher (it is true of parent as well) has of course his own inner universe. The difficulty is that it was, like the student's, largely shaped in his early formative and adolescent years, under exposure to a different set of events and experiences and changes from those of the student. The dislocation of values in recent decades has come from a failure of teacher and parent to bridge the distance between their inner universe and that of the young. It was a failure of values communication, an absence of a values dialogue.

Placing side by side the clusters of traditional and challenger values, one notes a calendar of rejections, accompanied by an effort at replacement.

There was a rejection of the political-economic cluster: *money, power, success, prestige, security* (the "five-goal system" as it was called in the 1950s). In its place the challenger system tried to move out of the economic culture, get free of the "rat race," and find its own forms of power and prestige and its own inner security. The swing went too far however, and covered not only the *success-and-competition* syndrome, which had become overblown, but also the *work ethos,* and with it what formed part of the same cluster—*self-discipline, career effort, achievement.*

There was a rejection of *authority* in most of its institutional forms, especially in politics, law, the family, and the older generation. In its place came an effort to find new forms of *personal credibility,* and a search for *authenticity* ("doing your own thing") rather than authority. This was all to the good, but *"anything goes"* proved no substitute for *consensual codes,* and the young found that even their communes couldn't get along without the shaping of new authority. There was a rejection of *power* in every institution, not only military and war power but most forms of state and economic power. In its place the challenger culture reached for a *radical libertarianism* which was reminiscent of some of the anarchist thinkers like Henry David Thoreau and Benjamin Andrews.

There was a rejection of pretty much the whole cluster of traditional sexual values, including all the Puritan virtues and taboos, and postponed gratification, and the idea of normal sex as against the perversions. This had healthy elements in it. But instant gratification, casualness about sexuality, and (again) the "anything goes" slogan did damage to the relation of intimacy and the love commitment. Similarly the rejection of masculine domination and of ascribed women's roles was healthy, but with it came the danger of diminishing the inward sense of masculine and feminine identity and the resulting historic balance between the sexes. There was a healthy rejection of the idea of one life-style to which everybody had to conform, and a flowering of diverse life-styles which may prove one of the lasting impacts of the challenger culture. There was a rejection of hypocrisies in every form, and a healthy stress on openness and honesty. There was similarly a healthy rejection of the constricted personality, and a stress on relaxed life rhythms, closeness to the soil, warmth of bodily contact, awareness of self and the other.

This calendar of rejections and replacements could be extended considerably. But I have dealt with some of the major value clusters, and given some of my own subjective judgments on the rejections, the challenges, and the changes, in order to suggest the core process at work in the values revolution.

The challenger groups had two crucial allies. One was the working of peer-group relationships, with a

contagion or mimesis principle which gave them a
sense of confidence as against the traditional values
system. The other was the media, with which the
challengers formed a curious love-hate relation, despising TV as technology yet watching it endlessly
and working with it; despising the press yet reveling
in its publicity, and developing an underground press
of their own; latching on to the camera, in photography
and movies, as their most cherished and characteristic
art form, developing their own underground films and
capturing even the commercial movies for a high
acceptance of pornography.

If the family and the school were evicted from the
educational premises of the young, one might say that
the media were taken on as new tenants, expressing
and enhancing some of the challenger values, and
acting as multiplier for them.

I have dealt above with the dynamics of value
changes in the culture, which ought to be one of the
chief concerns of education but, alas, has not been.
I move from this to the intricate processes by which
values are shaped, internalized, transmitted, transformed.

The Natural History of Value Formation

How do values get formed? I suggest that there
are a series of seven phases of the process that can
be considered separately, although they run together
as a continuum. I set them down here all too schemati-
cally.

1) *Exposure* to a values situation, or scenario. These
exposures begin in early childhood. Students of the
cognitive growth in the child, like Piaget and Bruner,
while not studying values as such, have prepared a
groundwork on which related studies of the earliest
exposure to values situations could build. There are
values agents, or actors, in these values situations,
whether at home, school, playground, or in the street.
The exposures at the earliest age are like being thrown

into the water: the values agents and models must help the child to swim.

I might add that the exposure process doesn't end with childhood, but that a continuing sequence of exposures goes on all through the life history. I add also that values exposure is not the same as values conditioning, which is the setting up of a particular values environment in order to get a particular response.

2) *Identification* with particular values agents or models in the values situation, such as parent, sibling, teacher, schoolmate, friend, authority figure, media figure. This identification is likely (although not necessarily) to be stronger with a primary values agent (father, sister, brother, close friend) than with a secondary one (political or media hero).

In each case there is an affective filament of linkage. Objectively—it is rarely conscious or explicit—it would run: "I want to behave in the manner of X, and make the choices X makes because I want to be like X." It becomes a species of friendly magic, a genial sorcery, operating by contagion and mimesis, as if the identifier expected the *mana* of the values model to become part of him.

The basic process I describe here is repeated all through life, the models varying with the life situations, from parent, sibling, teacher, to lover, spouse, priest or pastor, guru, charismatic leader, and even (by a reverse twist) one's child, when grown. The widespread and widely noted erosion of heroes and heroism today may be seen as the depletion of the capacity for model identification as the affective life grows weaker and the filament of linkage gets broken.

I need scarcely say that the growth of a severe antiseptic rationalism, especially in the intellectual community, has played havoc with the identification phase of values formation. This is especially true in adolescence, when a values vacuum can wreak almost as much havoc in the form of anomie as the absence of a loving adult can wreak in earliest infancy arresting the life force. In the 1950s teachers found that it was the absentee father—absent on business and career— who produced the identification model vacuum. In the 1970s it is more likely to be the absentee mother— absent in factory or office or career pursuit.

In any phase of the life history there is likely to be one from among a number of value agents who is the effective model for that phase. Let us call him or her the value ideal. I suspect that in the less complex—and less sensation-battered—society of the earlier republic the identification in childhood and adolescence with the value ideal was effected with a classic simplicity, without the obstructions and distortions that clog it today.

3) *Encounter, confrontation, choice.* These are closely linked with the identification phase, and with each other. If we take William Faulkner's story, *The Bear,* as a case history, we have an archetypal example of an adolescent in an encounter with a memorable situation, confronting (wrestling with) it, and making a choice which flows directly from his father's image as value ideal. Faulkner's nostalgia for a lost society and a lost world of childhood, and his preoccupation with the symbolic enactments in growing up, makes his writing a treasure-trove for values theory. This is true also of Hemingway's feeling for the rites of passage in the life history, right up to the *Old Man and the Sea,* where the encounter was with the primal force of the old man's life, and the value ideal was his self-image, accumulated from past values encounters and choices.

The problem today is that the encounters occur in fragmented situations, the confrontations are not ritualized, and the choices are made by contact with what may be a confusing array of models. Where in an earlier society the functions of work, play, learning, loving, and worshiping were all of a piece, there is now a separation of the work place, the learning place,

the play place, and the loving place, while the worshiping place tends to get left out. This makes the
process of values choice harder.

4) *Validation.* The values choices, when first made,
are tentative. They need to be validated if they are
to take on the force of authority. It is true not only
of the childhood and adolescent years but throughout
life that we need to have our values choices checked
and rechecked, even when they first came out of
identification with a values ideal. Values learned in
the family or school had to be validated in the peer
group, even in Mark Twain's society. His understanding of the processes of peer group validation makes
Huckleberry Finn a key book on American education,
as important for its time as Rousseau's *Emile* had
been a century earlier in Europe. The fact that the
father has been an authority figure in the American
family and the mother a humanist figure, the culture-
carrier, made values choice and validation easier than
they are today, when the trend is to scrap differential
role playing between the parents.

I use the term *validation* rather than Skinner's
reenforcement, just as earlier I used *exposure* rather
than *conditioning. Reenforcement* implies a *someone*
who arranges the reenforcing situation. *Validation*
is part of the whole probing and exploring process
by which we grow. It is in that sense democratic,
where *reenforcement* is authoritarian.

5) *Internalizing.* This is the process of making the
value choice part of oneself, not necessarily in a
conscious way, but in a deep internal way, so that
it becomes a habitual and unreflecting—almost a
reflexive—way of meeting a situation. In his thinking
on will and habit, William James sounds old-fashioned
today in his stress on using will to turn moral choices
into deliberately practiced, habitual ones. He was
making explicit what happens in more spontaneous
ways in the internalizing of values. Justice Holmes
described the end-product of this process when he

spoke of his life philosophy as a number of *can't helps*. David Riesman's use of the term *inner-orientation* also describes the end-product of internalizing. How we move toward it and how we get there is harder to describe.

6) *Ritualizing, sacrilizing.* This is a later and more intensive form of internalizing. The work ethic became a ritual, almost an addiction, as did the money ethic. They were no longer values pursued for some life-purpose but became purposes in themselves. This was true of a number of the sexual values as well, notably premarital chastity and the masculine domination of the family. My term *sacrilizing* is another way of looking at the same process, as with love of country as a value, or godliness. In both ritualizing and sacrilizing the values took on a mystique which exempted them from critical analysis and a rigidity which weakened them in the end.

7) *Challenge, scrutiny, replacement.* This is the last phase of one values cycle which becomes the first phase of another. I described in the preceding section, on the values revolution, how the credibility of values weakens when new currents of generational experience are not reckoned with in values transmission. It happened in the 1960s, which formed a decade of intense critical scrutiny of values that suffered a loss of authority and were desacrilized. When this happens on a wide front it raises the question not only of the viability of particular values but of the value system as a whole.

Splittings and Healings: Reflections on the Life Cycle

There are two crucially different, although related, ways of looking at the life cycle. One is to ask—as Freud, Piaget, and Erikson have done—what are the psychic characteristics of each of its sequence of stages. The second is to ask—as very few have done—what is the optimal sequence of life exposures and values shaping for the successive stages: given what we know about the psychic needs and energies at each stage, what kind of life and values experience is best reached for at that stage, and what should education focus on?

There are a number of possible approaches to this. My own is to start with the splittings that we observe in the characteristic life history in American society, to stress the need for healings and wholeness all through the life history, and to suggest at what stages the current gaps in the wholeness of the educational arts can best be repaired.

Let us say, with Shakespeare, that there are seven ages of man—and woman. Let us call them infancy, childhood, adolescence (to 18), early manhood and womanhood (19 to 29), early middle age (30 to 44), later middle age (45 to 64), the aging and concluding years (65 on). I have stretched the middle years here at both ends, starting them earlier and ending them later (middle 60s) than in most formulations, in part because the medical arts and self-knowledge have stretched the years of vigor, in part because anxieties and values confusion set in earlier than we had thought.

Everything we have been learning about the psychic aspects of the life pilgrimage point to the third (adolescence), fifth and sixth (early and later middle years) as the confused and explosive phases. Educators have done considerable thinking about adolescence, since the high school and early college years form the classic period of cognitive educational experience. They have done a good deal less on the other two, when presumably the educational job is all done, for better or worse. Yet if we take the view that education is for the whole life, and add that the decade from the early 30s to the early 40s is probably as explosive as adolescence, and that the stretch following it can turn either into decline or into the fullness of one's powers, then some rethinking is in order.

First, some observations about adolescence. Its na-

ture is best revealed in terms of paradox and contradiction. It is a time of rapid strides—physically,
sexually, intellectually, emotionally—yet it is also a
time of moratorium, of waiting and dawdling. It is
filled with intense longings, yearnings, dreamings, but
also with frustrations. It is a time when pent-up
energies clamor for release, but also one of passivity,
of gawking, of hesitating on the brink of action. It
is a time of hunting in single-sex packs, of huddling
for warmth in closeness of the male or female bond,
but it is also a time of cross-sexual exploration, of
reaching for intimate relations with outward boldness
but inner timidity. It is a time of dawning scepticism,
when earlier love-objects or identification models have
lost their hold, but it is also a time of hunger for
something or someone to believe in and hold on to.
It is a time for dreaming of honor, achievement, fame,
but also one of searching for an anodyne (alcohol,
drugs) which will ease the terrible adolescent sadness
of life, break the dullness of the school years, and
offer dreams against a reality that turns out differently
from the ideal.

What educators have done with these years of a
raw, wonderful openness has been to make them primarily the years of schooling, with classroom work
as the core. In theory, at least, these have been years
of cognitive burdens, as if the educators were driving
toward a kind of Piagetian fulfillment. For some ado-
lescents it has worked. For many others—physically
restless, classroom-confined, value-confused, unpre-
pared by family background for what seems irrelevant
information and abstractions—it has been in practice
a torture to be avoided when possible and ended at
the earliest chance. The junior high and high school
years are considered, by common consent, the problem
years of schooling, and their world has become a
wasteland of boredom and dropouts.

A word about the next stage, through the late 20s
of early manhood and womanhood. For· many it is

the best phase, provided they have tolerably survived the confused years of adolescence. They move out expansively toward the mastery of a craft which will open a job or career to them, and toward the intimacy of married sexuality and the start of a family. The home-leaving years give way to home-making, for young men as well as young women.

This sense of budding mastery and of hope is what makes the explosive years of the 30s and early 40s more poignantly crisis-ridden. In many, perhaps most, cases the promise doesn't lead to fulfillment. Value questions return. As Daniel Levinson puts it, there is a struggle between incompatible drives—for stability and for explorations of freedom, for career and for greater life adventures. Life becomes question-riddled, as it was in adolescence. Marriages get rocky, and both husband and wife grow absorbed with sexual and identity probings.

I have two interrelated approaches to suggest to the understanding of these problems of the life cycle in America. One has to do with the psychosocial splittings which help to account for the confusions of this stretch from early adolescence into mid-life. The other has to do with aspects of wholeness in a person, whose understanding may help in healing the splits.

To be very brief about the first, which I have repeatedly touched on in the preceding pages: There was a greater wholeness about life in the earlier republic, especially in the traditional cultures of rooted small-town and small-city living, than there is today. We live in an age of uprootings, separations, splittings, broken connections, which tend to fragment the wholeness of the growing person or prevent the wholeness from being achieved.

This is the Great Transformation of American life. Its crisis came at the turn of the century, with revolutions of technology, especially of transportation, with the breakaway from the rural society and the rise of the big city, with the breaking up of the extended family. The crisis was renewed at the time of World War I, and again with the New Deal and World War II, and decisively in the late fifties and through the sixties. But James and Dewey, in their day, were already generalizing from a society that had in effect vanished, and would never return.

The rooted values of the traditional ethos came out of an economy which carried a belief system with it. But with the splittings a cultural climate was shaped which found the economy—and the business culture which sustained it—dehumanizing and unjust, and rejected the means by which we live. This in turn was applied to other institutions of the society— technology, the family, the school, the church, the government.

One can use as watershed the great work of Josef Schumpeter, *Capitalism, Socialism, and Democracy,* published in the early 1940s, which generalized both from the experience of the Weimar Republic and that of American social democracy. Schumpeter saw what James and Dewey had failed to see—the irrational elements from the new culture which had been turned against the institutions of the society, the strong rejections, the sense of shame and guilt among the young about the achievements of their parents. He saw the ironic probability that they would rise against capitalist democracy because of its successes, not its failures. What he failed to see was that their skepticisms about institutions converged with their self-doubts and values confusions, and came not only out of the so-cial uprootings but out of the splinterings of their wholeness.

The ritual enactments of the rebellion against the father, the need for individual identity, the leaving of home, the effort to find and found a new one and to complete the eternal recurrence of generations, has been repeated constantly with each generation but under more difficult life situations. One may speak of a number of recurring and related binds from adolescence into mid-life—the rational-irrational bind, the Puritan-pleasure bind, the career-adventure bind, the stability-roaming bind, the belief-skepticism bind. Unless we understand the splits and binds I have discussed, we shall not be able to use our vast educational resources for healing and wholeness.

My second approach moves toward education from the starting-point of the aspects of wholeness of living and being. We have mostly stressed two aspects in our educational thinking—man working and man thinking (or learning). Let us call them *homo faber* and *homo cogitans* (or *homo cognoscens*). There are several others. There are man playing (*homo ludens*), man loving (*homo amans*), man governing (*homo gubernans* or *homo civis*), man wandering and exploring (*homo ambulans*), man praying (*homo sacer*). The Latinisms are not important, and I use them only because *homo faber* and *homo ludens* have become a familiar part of the literature of education. But the functions and aspects of total living that they designate *are* important; man at work, as producer; man at play, and in the world of the arts; man as thinker, coping with concepts and abstractions; man immersed in the erotic and generative, and suffused with it; civic man, governing and being governed; man the explorer, wandering the earth and among the planets, restless and roaming; man the reverent, involved with worship and the godhead.

One thing that strikes me sharply, as I approach the end of this essay in the theory and arts of applying values to education, is how little we have heeded the need for the convergence of all of these aspects of the developing man, the developing woman. (Obviously I have used the *homo* terms above, for simplicity, but have meant them to apply generically to women as well as men.)

We need to rethink the life cycle within this context. Play is crucial in childhood, where we tend to localize it, but it is crucial also in the rest of the life history, from which we have excluded it. Classroom study, for work and career and for molding civic man, is crucial in the childhood and adolescent years, where we have localized it. But manual and craft skills are as important as the cognitive ones in these early stages, and we do a disservice to human development by downgrading them, and thus giving many youngsters of high school and college age a sense that they are failures and misfits if they choose to follow the manual and craft bent. In fact we should—from the start—interweave manual and craft training with the cognitive, bring youngsters into the offices and factories and technical laboratories for work-study programs, and bring workers, craftsmen, technicians, and businessmen into the school system so as to get the work-study-career continuum that Willard Wirtz has written about.

We need also to bring in exploring. To counter the drop-out effect, which is a pathetic form of exploring, we need to encourage the present tendency of young people to go out from school and home into the world of travel, adventure, jobs, sexuality, so that they can interweave the idea and the act and—as it were—*actualize* themselves and their place in the society. This will mean a postponement of the settled-down professional study and career and home. But when they return, after several wanderings, they will be better prepared for becoming generative man and civic man and sacral man. They will be prepared for an acceptance of the rational father principle in the society, and for an acceptance of self as well.

The Eros principle is crucial in education, using Eros to mean both the sexual core and the life affirmation that goes with it when it is expressive. So is the sacral principle, *homo sacer.* Those who are for some form of religious study in the school are usually against the study of sexuality, and those who favor the latter tend to oppose the former. I happen to think that both have been badly done, but also that both are necessary—preferably with a crucial continuity between the home and school, so that parental wounds will not be reopened.

In what I have said of the other six aspects of growth and wholeness I have not intended to underplay the cognitive. In fact, I feel it is now overstressed in the early years and then dropped in the later ones. It should be a continuing theme of growth, into the later mid-years and the aging decades, along with love and exploration and play, so that older people will have not a sense of closures but a feeling of renewal.

A Democratic Elite and a Values Synthesis

In every educational system the question of *elite* and *demos* is a plaguing one: shall the major thrust of the system be toward the select (or elect—that is to say, elite) or the demos, the people? In past societies few would doubt that it was the former. In contemporary societies few would dare say it was anything but the latter. The truth is—at least for modern industrial and democratic societies—that it is a mischievous and unrewarding question. A better one to ask is how we can best make a synthesis of both aims by a values dialogue between the best of both groups.

Nietzsche, in a series of lectures as a young docent and later embodying his insights in some of his early writing, had a scornful and unequivocal answer. The main purpose of education was neither for the state nor the people, nor was it for the new middle classes. It was, as I have noted earlier, to nourish and sustain geniuses. He was fascinated with the Greek *agon*, as he was with the primitive energies the Greeks brought to every pursuit, and their Dionysian zest for excess and transcendence. He scorned the ideal of the German state and the modern democracies, to turn out safely mediocre citizens for home and country.

American democracy has little use for the Nietzsche-an superman ideal. But the Greek ideal of excellence, and that of the Renaissance, were part of the interplay of activities among the American aristocracies of the eighteenth century as they pursued fighting, riding, governing, law, oratory, the classics. American history has not lacked for aristocracies: landowning, military, political, legal, industrial, intellectual. The problem was what their role should be in a democracy in relation to the people themselves, the *demos,* and what the functions of education should be for both. As part of the European Enlightenment, the America of Thomas Jefferson and John Adams stood on the threshold of a democratic era, but it had not left the aristocratic one behind.

In his classic letter to John Adams, of October 28, 1813, Jefferson—despite the myths that have gathered around him—envisaged popular government in America within the framework of a governing elite which was a natural aristocracy whose grounds were "virtue and talent." He was confident that the property holders in America, as also those with "comfortable subsistence" and a "satisfactory situation" in life, would—unlike "the canaille of the cities of Europe"—advantageously reserve to themselves a wholesome control over their public affairs." Even in Europe he saw science, talents, and courage beginning to triumph over wealth and birth. But his real affirmation was that for America "that form of govenment is the best which provides most effectually for a pure selection of these natural aristoi into the offices of government."

This is still a democratic ideal, but it is the ideal of a democratic elite, deriving not from birth or privilege but from the people themselves, subject to the competition of ability, energy, and character, and granting the rewards of office, authority, and the good life to those who show their mettle and quality in this rivalry. It is not the meritocracy of clerks and technicians which Michael Young pilloried in *The Rise of the Meritocracy,* but neither is it the quota democracy of George McGovern's 1972 Democratic

convention, which operated by the statistical corre-
lates of population distribution. It provides for as good
a synthesis of the talents of the elites and the rough,
creative strength of the people as most human arrange-
ments are likely to achieve.

The balancing of interests between a democratic
elite and a popular majority is one that can in time
be resolved. The more difficult task of educating the
young people whose talents make them the carriers
of promise, and at the same time educating those who
are a good distance away from a comfortable subsistence, will be harder, but the dialogue between them
is bound to strengthen each. Nor are there insur-
mountable problems in finding ways of renewing the
strength of the democratic elite itself. We now know
(see Kluger) that in planning the strategy of *Brown*
v. *Board of Education* the legal-intellectual elites of
both whites and blacks combined to afford a new
access to the elite groups for the sons and daughters
of the black *demos.* Thus the achievement of an
egalitarian goal can become an instrument for replen-
ishing an elite with new vigor from below.

A problem more difficult than any of the above
occurs in a democracy when the elites themselves grow
bitter and alienated, and use their talents destructively.
Jefferson foresaw the dangers of a *canaille.* He did
not foresee the emergence of elites characterized by
the sense of guilt or boredom of the sons and daughters
of the possessors. The characteristic elites of our time
are those of anomie as well as those of fanatic violence.
In every case the *talent* is there. But the *virtue?*
Jefferson's use of the term "virtue" as the purposes
of individual and collective living which the talents
must serve, presents a central issue of education as
a values instrument.

There have been alternations in history of the values
profiles of the young Americans who are likely to
become members of the democratic elite. My own
experience as a teacher on college campuses may be

of interest here. My student generation of the 1930s was very socially conscious, sharing the hope and militancy of the New Deal and often going beyond it. My students of the 1940s generation were both career-oriented and inner-oriented, since that was the time of the spread of a kind of high Freudianism in America. My students of the 1950s were largely apathetic and socially unconscious—bent on the conformity which would enable them to "make it" along with others. My students of the 1960s were again very socially conscious, involved in political activisms and in the revolutions of the counter-culture.

The values situation among the young today is that of an interregnum. The traditional ethos was for a time badly mauled, although it has shown considerable resilience. A challenger ethos emerged, and continues to exert an appeal, but is still the possession of a minority and has yet to prove its fruitfulness to the middle-middle and lower-middle strata. The young are commuting between the two worlds, not quite belonging to either, and they are perforce practicing an operational ethos which is characteristically theirs.

A strong light is shed on them by several attitude studies of campus values by Daniel Yankelovich. He noted a shift, at the start of the seventies, from the intense activism of the sixties to a new "naturalism" of values. This would confirm my own hypothesis, noted earlier, that the counter-culture will prove more enduring than the activist ones and that its rooted aspects—the feeling about the land, ecology, the simple, the authentic—is a counter-force to its irrational aspect. But it is only one phase of a complex emerging orientation.

There is a renewed interest in study and also in jobs and careers—which gives a reentry into the work ethic. In the political area the liberal-radical attitudes continue, although somewhat abated. But a stronger trend is a deep cynicism about political institutions, with an almost paranoid sense that intrigue and conspiracy are part of the web of government, and that public life is a rigged game. This does not however reach to an apathy about politics. There is still a feeling—not as pronounced as in the mid-40s—that one can work within the system and make it less squalid. As with politics there is little outright idealism among those planning to go into the professions, yet there is far less of the aggrandizing intent than in the past. The young want to be doctors, but not to neglect the public health aspect, to be lawyers but not to omit advocacy law, to be architects and engineers but not to ignore public projects and city planning.

A similar eclectic, synthesizing effect shows itself in other areas—in religion (elements of the occult, the psychedelic, the traditional church-going, along with a dash of Fundamentalism in the "Jesus movement"); in sexuality (a greater acceptance of school-age sex and of the pill and abortion, with a greater casualness about it and few of their parents' hang-ups); about love and family (less of romantic love, more of a combination of comradeship and a quiet sort of commitment, whether in marriage or pair-bond relationships); about narcotics (continued use of grass, less hard drugs, a return to the parental alcohol and tobacco); about life-styles (continuance of the jeans-and-sleeping-bag mode of traveling lightly in life, changes in pairing until a right partner is found, greater interest in women's quality and independence, eagerness of young women for careers but without giving up marriage and children as prime goals).

Since the values generations of the young have become briefer, and the changing of the guard more rapid, it is idle to expect that the profile I have sketched out will be an enduring one. But its broad directions are likely to last for a time, as also its basic bind. The bind lies in the still unresolved tension between polar values: to work hard *and* to be casual; to make a living *and* to make a life; to reject materialism *and* to afford travel, technology, and gadgetry; to be free for personal growth *and* to raise children well; to be open to adventure *and* to be committed to continuing love and family loyalties; to care about country (patriotism is no longer as square as it was) *and* to be a citizen of the world; to explore new modes of consciousness and awareness *and* to continue embracing the everyday pragmatisms of life.

I have spoken mostly of the campus young, who are the vanguard value carriers, yet their binds and resolutions are not very different from those of their elder compeers in their 20s and 30s and even of the later life-stages. Americans are diverse in their life situations, and are pluralist in their life-styles, but they are joined in common characteristic binds if not by common bonds.

This is the reality that teacher, parent, and adviser must deal with in their work of value forming and values resolution. It will be seen as a more possible task if we understand that, in the dialectical process, what appears from one angle of vision as a bind is from another angle of vision the phase of antithesis, preceding the stage of synthesis. In the dialectic of value change the new generation tries to live in both worlds which are in conflict within it, to extract the best from each and discard the rest, to have its moral cake *and* eat it.

It gets help in this process from the fact that the history of values change moves in cyclical swings. The sixties were a little like the thirties in their values, the seventies are a little like the forties, but the cyclical swing doesn't return to its starting point, like the Oriental image of the serpent with its tail in its mouth. It returns, but from a different angle, at a different level. Moreover, a cultural organism, like an individual one, constantly seeks equilibrium, even among its continuing storms. After the rapid accelerations of change in the sixties, after the decelerations of the seventies, the inner world of values seeks a homeostasis and it may find it in an emerging values synthesis.

Each of the opposing value systems—the traditional and the challenger—contains nourishing and un- nourishing value clusters, rooted and uprooted ones. The constricted and repressive values of the Puritan ethos—the sexual stringency cluster, the respectable morality cluster, the male dominance cluster, the success-and-materialism cluster—have been subjected to a withering attack. But the cluster of individual worth and independence, of self-reliance and self- discipline, of work and achievement, of merit and reward, of roots in the soil and the local community, of due process of law and equality before the law, of civic religion, of the valuing of children, growth, and education—these rooted values still have a deep strength. One can make the same point in comparing the far-out, alienated, and extremist values of the counter-culture (purgative violence, the drug mys- tique, the flight from science and history, the denial of detachment, the battle-cry of "anything goes" in pornography and in activist protest) with the rooted values (spontaneity, simplicity, the "roots in the land" cluster, the antihypocrisy cluster, the awareness and transcendence cluster, the transpersonal cluster, the extended family cluster)—and again one gets a set of values strains with a deep strength in them.

If we could put together the rooted values from each ethos they would not only be compatible: they would have a deep affinity for each other. Anyone studying the emergence of the challenger culture is likely to find that its vanguard carriers often used different names for the same basic values as the traditional ethos, and discovered different routes for getting at them.

The real question is not whether a synthesis, once achieved, would hold together: it is whether it can be achieved, and whether our educational resources are up to the task of helping to effect it. There is a difference between a values synthesis and a political consensus. The latter results largely from the give-

and-take in the marketplace of the party system and
the media. A values synthesis operates more privately
and indirectly, in the mind and psyche, although
through the agency largely of the home, the school,
the media.

Yet these agencies do have on their side the Eros
principle, in its broadest meaning. For Freud, who
used it in his later writings in opposition to the death
principle (Thanatos), it was more than the pleasure
principle. It was life affirmation, the life force. It is
the ultimate stuff of all educational striving, as it is
of all human striving. But to be able to tap it, the
values agents must start with the inner universe and
life situation of the student, not with their own. They
must start with the student's environments, including
the family.

But if they hope to find some seeds of the Eros
principle in the student and his situation, they must
bring the seeds of their own to the teaching-learning
experience. "Mirror, mirror, on the wall," reads a
cartoon caption in an issue of the *Kappan*. "Who is
the most sensitive, open, student-centered, and inno-
vative teacher of them all?" The teacher is standing
before the mirror, preening himself on his up-to-
dateness. This is how once living ideas become fash-
ionable and rigid—and get caricatured. Yet it is true
of the effective teacher that he must have some elements in him both of *magus* and *magister.*

If the teacher does, then the classroom can become
a joyful classroom, instead of an angry or bleakly dull
one. The teacher-student relation, if it is to be creative,
must go through the stages of encounter, exploration,
crisis, and transcendence, as every other creative relation does. If the teacher can take an affirmative view
of the media, understanding that they can be not a
mechanical agent but a living force in the lives of
his students and in the classroom itself, he will be
recruiting a strong resource for the learning process.
And if he can use the student's own life situation

and the experience of the culture as case histories in the winnowing and critical examination of values, he will be playing the magical role of the values catalyst. If he can see through some of his own values cast, and present confidently to the student the values that have survived his own scrutiny, there can be a values dialogue and a values exchange between them. In the end education is nothing much more than such a values dialogue.

Out of these values encounters will come in time something closer than we have today to a values elite—one that takes the lead in both the change and continuity of values and becomes a force for contagion in spreading them, in a larger dialogue with the people themselves.

Thus out of chaos—in Nietzsche's phrase—the teacher and the student together can fashion a dancing star.

Notes on Reading

I set down a small selection from the books that have been helpful in my thinking on education and values:

On Rousseau and Nietzsche: Jean-Jacques Rousseau, *Emile*, many editions; Friedrich Nietzsche, *The Nietzsche Portable*, ed. by Walter Kaufmann (Viking, 1954).

On James and Dewey: William James, *Principles of Psychology* (Dover, 1890) and *Talks to Teachers on Psychology and to Students on Some of Life's Ideals* (Dover, 1899); John Dewey, *The Early Works of John Dewey, 1882-1898*, ed. by Jo Ann Boydston, 5 vols. (Southern Illinois University Press, 1975); John Dewey, *Experience and Education* (Macmillan, 1963).

On Marx: *Karl Marx on Education, Women, and Children*, ed. by S. K. Padover (McGraw-Hill, 1975).

On Freud and the psychoanalytic schools: Sigmund Freud, *Civilization and Its Discontents* (Anchor, 1958); Otto Rank, *Modern Education: A Critique of Its Fundamental Ideas* (Agathon Press, 1968); Alfred Adler, *Understanding Human Nature* (Fawcett, 1968).

On other aspects of the psychology of education: B. F. Skinner, *Beyond Freedom and Dignity* (Knopf, 1971); A. T. W. Simeons, *Man's Presumptuous Brain* (Dutton, 1962); Richard L. Evans, *Jean Piaget—The Man and His Ideas: A Dialogue with Piaget* (Dutton, 1973); Jerome Bruner, *The Process of Education* (Harvard, 1960), *On Knowing* (Harvard, 1962), and *Toward a Theory of Instruction* (Harvard, 1966); Maya Pines, *Revolution in Learning: The Years from Birth to Six* (Harper, 1966); Abraham Maslow, *Toward a Psychology of Being* (rev. ed., Nostrand, 1968), and *The Farther Shores of the Mind* (Viking, 1972); Saul Harrison and John McDermott, eds., *Childhood Psychopathology: An Anthology of Basic Readings* (International University, 1972).

A cluster on ethnology and the human inheritance: Konrad Lorenz, *On Aggression* (Harcourt, 1966); and Richard Evans, *Konrad Lorenz: The Man and His Ideas* (Harcourt, 1975); Robert Ardrey, *The Hunting Hypothesis* (Atheneum, 1976); Anthony Storr, *Human Destructiveness* (Basic, 1972); Erich Fromm, *The Anatomy of Human Destructiveness* (Fawcett, 1975); John Belibtreu, *The Parable of the Beast* (Macmillan, 1968).

On the history of American education and educators: Lawrence A. Cremin, *American Education, The Colonial Experience*

(Harper, 1970), and *The Transformation of the School: Progressivism 1876-1957* (Knopf, 1961); Merle Curti, *The Social Ideas of American Educators* (Littlefield, 1959); Jonathan Messerli, *Horace Mann: A Biography* (Knopf, 1972); Fred and Grace Hechinger, *Growing Up in America* (McGraw-Hill, 1975).

On education and the life cycle: Richard I. Evans, *Dialogue with Erik Erikson* (Harper, 1967); William Irwin Thompson, *Passages About Earth: An Exploration of the New Planetary Culture* (Harper, 1974).

On intelligence, inequality, and the meritocracy: Ken Richardson and David Spears, eds., *Race and Intelligence* (Penguin, 1972); Arthur R. Jensen, *Educability and Group Differences* (Harper, 1973); Christopher Jencks, *Inequality: A Reassessment of the Effect of Family and Schooling in America* (Basic, 1972); Michael Young, *The Rise of the Meritocracy, 1870-2033: An Essay on Education and Equality* (Gannon, 1959); Nathan Glazer, *Affirmative Discrimination: Ethnic Inequality and Public Policy* (Basic, 1976).

On opening up the schools: Ewald B. Nyquist and Gene R. Hawes, eds., *Open Education: A Source Book* (Bantam, 1972); Charles E. Silberman, ed., *The Open Classroom Reader* (Vintage, 1973); Neil Postman and Charles Weingartner, *The School Book: For People Who Want to Know What All the Hollaring Is About* (Delacorte, 1973), and *Teaching as a Subversive Activity* (Delacorte, 1969).

On the government of education: Alan Rosenthal, ed., *Governing Education* (Anchor, 1969).

On talented children, Michael Deakin, *The Children on the Hill* (Bobbs Merrill, 1972); John Hersey, *The Child Buyers* (Knopf, 1960).

On the work/learning continuum, Willard Wirtz, *The Boundless Resource* (New Republic, 1975).

On values: Milton Rokeach, *The Nature of Human Values* (Free Press, 1973); Daniel Yankelovich, *The Changing Values on Campus* (Pocket Books, 1972); Abraham Maslow, *Religions, Values, and Peak Experiences* (Ohio State, 1964).

Index

New Frontier—88
New Left—71-72
New Nationalism—88
New York—47
  New York City—86
Nietzsche, Friedrich—28, 82, 119, 127
Nisbet, Robert—80
Nixon, Richard—73
North Carolina—101
Novak, Michael—94

Old Man and the Sea—110
On Liberty—78
Organism, The—58

Parker, Theodore—11
Parrington, Vernon Lewis—52
Pavlov, Ivan—57
peer groups—4, 18, 76, 86, 107
Peirce, Charles—47-48
Pericles—79
Perls, Fritz—63-64
"People's Colleges"—12
Phi Delta Kappan—126
Phillips, Kevin—5
"Philosopher-King"—15
Piaget, Jean—57-58, 108, 112, 114
Plato—77
Platonic "Guardians"—65, 77
Poland
  Warsaw—87
political conservativism—16, 26, 53, 56, 61
political liberalism—26, 53, 61-62, 75, 85, 90-92
politics—15, 17, 56-79, 83-84
Populist Movement—48, 52, 88
Pound, Roscoe—52
pragmatism—16, 26, 47-48, 50, 54
Price, Richard—63
progressivism—39, 47-48, 52-53, 55, 72, 74, 85, 87
Protestant ethic—102
Prussia—77
psychoanalysis—46, 55, 59, 66